EDINBURGH CITY LIBRARIES

Please return/renew this item by the last date shown.
To renew quote your borrower number.

Writing

Sports Stories
that Sell

*How to make money from writing
about your favourite pastime*

JEREMY BUTLER

How To Books

First published by How To Books Ltd, 3 Newtec Place,
Magdalen Road, Oxford OX4 1RE, United Kingdom.
Tel: (01865) 793806. Fax: (01865) 248780.
email: info@howtobooks.co.uk
www.howtobooks.co.uk

British Library Cataloguing in Publication Data
A catalogue record for this book is available from the
British Library

Editing by Julie Nelson
Cartoons by Mike Flanagan
Cover design by Shireen Nathoo Design
Cover image PhotoDisc

Produced for How To Books by Deer Park Productions.
Typeset by Anneset, Weston-super-Mare, Somerset.
Printed and bound by Cromwell Press, Trowbridge,
Wiltshire.

NOTE: The material contained in this book is set out in
good faith for general guidance and no liability can be
accepted for loss or expense incurred as a result of
relying in particular circumstances on statements made in
this book. The law and regulations may be complex and
liable to change, and readers should check the current
position with the relevant authorities before making
personal arrangements.

Contents

List of Illustrations

Preface

Every weekend thousands of people participate in organised sports and each of those sporting events is of interest to newspapers throughout the country. They are keen to ensure their readers know all the details of sports in their community and are desperate for well-written reports. Whether you are a club secretary looking to improve the quality of your writing or a young hack looking to make it all the way to Wapping, this book is aimed at helping you achieve your goal. It is packed with advice from leading sports stars and editors and reading the following pages should ensure you know how to make contacts, find stories and write them up in an accepted newspaper style.

Unlike other instruction-type books this guide will also give you an insight into how the profession works, from revealing who to contact on a sports desk to showing how to fight it out with other journalists to get your share of the stories. Written in a style that places you in the field rather than the classroom, this book gives you pointers on what to do, while allowing you to adapt your own style within the parameters. Finding your own style is a necessity, as successful journalists do not roll off the production line but develop their own interview techniques and writing manner. With a checklist in each chapter to ram home the key points you will feel more confident about your writing and your approach to the profession.

I would like to thank all the sports stars and journalists who have kindly given their time to help me in writing this book plus my parents, Colin and Mary and Lindsey Martin for their support.

Jeremy Butler

1

Enjoying the Fun of the Chase

> 'I've always said there is a place for the press but they haven't dug it yet.'
>
> *Former Manchester United manager Tommy Docherty*

DREAM JOB OR CHORE?

The Spanish sun can be fearsome when you've spent the afternoon plodding up and down a Formula One pit lane, so I decided it was time for a drink. I popped into the Ferrari motorhome for a quick refuel and spotted Michael Schumacher looking ice cool, despite the heat, explaining some technicality to one of his mechanics. Perfect timing, I thought, as I mopped the sweat from my brow and waited for the great German to finish his chat and turn to me.

Perfect gentleman off the track as he is, Schumacher swung round and noticed me as I hit him with my first question and without fail he stopped to give me a reply. The same situation had happened only moments before as English driver Johnny Herbert had asked me to join him and even made me a typically English brew as we talked. Schumacher was as accommodating as ever and with the quotes in the bag I returned to the air-conditioned press lounge to write my piece and then sit back and enjoy the Spanish Grand Prix.

SPOILING THE ILLUSION

Sounds like a wonderful life being a sports journalist, doesn't it? And there are days when you wouldn't swap the job for any other in the world. In fact, if you believe all you hear, a career in the sports writing field means getting paid to jet around the world and drink lots of your favourite tipple while watching the odd game with the small matter of filing a few words as a penance for your sins.

The sunshine destinations of the Spanish Grand Prix or the World Cup in the Far East and the chance to chat over the finer points of the day's events with a top sporting star are hardly to be sniffed at. And of course there is always the expense account that allows you to drink and eat the finest cuisine and wine on offer wherever you go. What about the words? It must be great fun to sit down and concoct a masterpiece equal to John Betjeman in rhythm and Shakespeare in word play. There can't be a better way to spend your time than being a sports writer.

But if that is your picture of what the game is all about and you view sports writing as the perfect way to make a fortune before heading off to the hills, then forget it. Here are five jobs you won't get in an instant:

- Grand Prix correspondent
- cricket tour reporter
- top writer at the Cup Final
- *Sunday Times* sports columnist
- worldwide tennis correspondent.

There are great days in the job. There are the lucky souls who are invited to Twickenham to enjoy free food and drink before settling into top class seats for a Five Nations game. But the usual reality is a freezing wet night at Bury with a copy deadline that ends before the match you are watching and a set of players who, even if you could recognise them, would not give you the time of day.

Imagine waiting, as I have done, two hours for an interview with a top name sports star and getting only a five-word answer to the one question you have time to put to them before they are whisked away. Then imagine trying to write a 1,000-word feature around that one brisk quote. Think about how depressing it can be hoping your eighth phone call of the day to a third division football manager for a check on a player's fitness will get through to save you from the potential disaster of failing to fulfil an order.

This is what it's really all about. It is hard work, full of pitfalls and disappointments and a long way from the Des Lynam job you may expect to be holding down in two years' time. But when everything goes right and you've filed a great slab of copy on time and got an incisive interview from the player you are after, then it is the best job in the world.

WHY BE A SPORTS JOURNALIST?

There are five key reasons why sports journalism is for you. If you can say 'yes' to the following, look forward to the time of your life:

- You love sport.

- You love writing.

- You love socialising.

- You don't mind hardships.

- You don't mind giving up your free time.

Don't pick and choose, all five factors need a 'yes' or you will not fully enjoy a career with pen and pad in your hand.

Stars in your eyes

Sport is now big business and if you get a buzz from meeting famous people you are in for a treat. As a sports journalist you will gain access to some of the world's top stars, and as long as you don't stumble over your words, proffer stupid questions or insult them, it is likely you will be able to enjoy a decent conversation.

In my time I have had coffee with David Coulthard, listened to Paul Gascoigne apologise for numerous incidents and discussed the finer points of a rugby game with the England front row. And a freelance friend of mine even managed to fix up an interview with Brazilian superstar striker Ronaldo by making a couple of well-directed phone calls.

If you are quick of thought and sharp of tongue you will surprise yourself about who you can meet. Superstars do talk – after all, they are only human beings like you or me. They just have a little more talent than the rest of us.

Impress your friends

There are few jobs more likely to impress your sports-loving friends than the field you are about to enter into. Anyone interested in the game would love to be paid to sit in a great seat, watch a match and then talk to the stars afterwards.

Your friends will probably kill for the kind of gossip about transfer news and players' personal lives you will be privileged to and they will be envious when they see your name in print. Of course, they will argue about your view of the match and ask if you were at the same game, but as a professional watcher of sport your views will suddenly become valued and your opinions championed like never before.

DO YOU HAVE WHAT IT TAKES?

Having got this far in the chapter you must wonder what you've stumbled over. Sports journalism really does sound like the dream job. But to get to the heights I have described you have to slog through an awful amount of lows.

Here are my five worst moments:

- Standing in the pouring rain for two hours for a report that was never used.

- Seeing your big moment ruined by a mistake in your story caused by someone else.

- Sitting in hours of traffic to get to a game worth only one paragraph in a paper.

- Waiting three hours for an interview and then being told to get lost.

- Being snubbed by sports-playing friends for something you didn't write.

The bottom line is you are being paid to watch the sport you love and voice your own opinion on matters thousands of people find interesting. If you like sport, love writing and are prepared to get your hands and feet wet, then read on – for you, my friend, there are many treats in store.

CASE STUDIES

Andy dreams of glory

Ever since he was at school Andy has dreamt of being a football genius but unfortunately his skills have failed to match his dreams and he is forced to think about another career. He realises the best way to stay close to the game is to write about it. That way he will go to big games and meet his favourite stars. So he sets out to be a sports journalist.

Jane wants to spice up her life

Jane has been an English teacher for 15 years and is beginning to feel bored by the same old routine. She is looking for a new challenge. She still enjoys her writing and is a keen sportswoman who plays several racket games for local clubs. Jane decides to try to forge a fun sideline to her teaching career by finding work as a freelance sports writer.

CHECKLIST

1. Are you sure you want to be a sports writer for the right reasons?

2. Do you have the determination to succeed?

3. Have you got enough time to make a real go of it?

4. Will spending your days investigating your favourite sport spoil the fun of watching it?

2

Getting into Journalism

THE CONVENTIONAL ROUTE

Most of the journalists writing for national papers today have followed a conventional route into journalism. They have worked their way through the ranks and shown the desire and skill needed to make it to the top of their profession. This path begins with a National Council for Training of Journalists (NCTJ) course, but as pay is low in journalism, such a route is generally followed by people under 25. Don't worry if your age rules out this route, because later in the chapter I will explain other ways to break into the field.

A typical way to the top will be:

- NCTJ pre-entry course (see below)

- a news job on a weekly paper

- a sports job on a weekly paper

- a regional paper post

- a position on a national newspaper.

JOINING A UNION

If you believe the backing of a trade union will help you progress in your writing, contact the best known – the National Union of Journalists. Although stripped of much of the power it held in its heyday, the NUJ is still recognised as the leading journalism union. They welcome full-time journalists as well as student memberships and can offer advice on training and other matters concerning starting out in the trade. Contact them at the address given at the back of this book.

LEARNING THE TRADE

Direct entry

There are two ways to start training for a career in journalism. The first and best route financially is to convince a newspaper you are good enough to go on their training course where they will pay you and teach you. This is known as **direct entry**.

Newspaper groups running these courses are:

- The Trinity Group on (0191) 201 6043

- Midland Newspapers on (01902) 313131

- The Education Centre (formerly Westminster Press) on (01424) 435991.

You will be handed a two-year contract with a probationary period of six months. Your course time will be split up as follows:

- six months – probationary period

- block release course

- work experience

- NCTJ or NVQ exam.

Pre-entry courses
The other way is to get in touch with the NCTJ who help students educated up to A-level standard enjoy the necessary training needed to get a job on a newspaper. Courses are generally held at colleges accredited by the NCTJ. This route is known as **pre-entry**. The minimum qualifications you need to be accepted on a pre-entry course are five GCSE passes, but most successful applicants either have two A-levels or are university graduates. A qualification in English is vital.

Study time is divided between

- law

- public affairs

- newspaper journalism

- shorthand.

GETTING ON A COURSE

Direct entry
If it is the direct entry route you want, apply to the editor of the newspaper you wish to work for. Names and contact addresses can be found in the latest editions of *Willings Press Guide, The Writer's Handbook* or *The Writers and Artists Yearbook*, copies of which can be found in your local library.

Pre-entry

For the pre-entry course send a 9 × 4 stamped addressed envelope to the National Council for the Training of Journalists, Latton Bush Centre, Southern Way, Harlow, Essex CM18 7BL. Applicants who catch the eye of the NCTJ have to take a written test and pass an interview before being awarded a place.

Bypassing the qualification problem

If you do not want to take a degree but still want to ensure you can earn an interview for a place on the pre-entry course, it is best to sign up for one of the NCTJ's approved courses aimed at A-level students. Anyone who successfully completes the two-year course is given access to the selection procedure even if they lack the required qualifications.

Approved college courses are held at:

- Lambeth College, London

- Handsworth College, Birmingham

- Sheffield College

- Highbury College, Portsmouth

- Swansea College

- City of London Community College.

Addresses for all of these can be obtained from the NCTJ, whose address can be found at the back of this book.

SIGNING UP FOR A DISTANCE LEARNING COURSE

The NCTJ now offers correspondence courses for people unable to commit themselves to full-time education. The course can lead to an NVQ in Newspaper or Periodical Journalism so a discount of 23 per cent tax relief at source can be offered to individuals.

The Foundation Course in Newspaper Journalism

This course covers the entire NCTJ syllabus except central government and takes three to six months to complete. It consists of:

- 15 units of self-assessed work

- a video on interviewing techniques

- eight audio tapes.

Writing for the Periodical Press

This course is aimed at people interested in writing for magazines found on the shelves of WHSmith and provides a base for writers planning a full-time career in magazine journalism. The work is spread over 10 modules and takes three to six months to complete. It covers:

- writing news and features

- sub-editing

- layout

- media law.

For information and the cost of both courses, phone (01279) 430009.

OTHER WAYS INTO JOURNALISM

You don't need to undertake a course to find your way into print. The rest of this chapter will show you other ways. But before the big day you dream about, when you pick up a paper and see your name in it, there is a long way to go.

TRAINING YOURSELF

Just because you don't fit into the criteria laid down by the NCTJ to go on one of their courses, do not think everything is lost. You can train yourself with a little dedication and a lot of hard work. Admittedly you will not have the knowledge of newspaper law and central government, but if you can write you will still find work.

'I take the Gucci view about hard work on the practice field. Long after you've forgotten the price, the quality remains.'
Aussie rugby coach Alan Jones

Practising to make perfect

'The more I practise the luckier I get.'

That is the gospel according to famous golfer Gary Player and it relates to your hobby as well. The more practice you put in, the better your writing will be and the luckier you will be in finding work.

You see, no matter how good a writer you are, it is impossible to think you can turn up one day and begin writing top copy for a sports desk. For a start when it comes to writing copy for newspapers all the rules you learnt about English during your school days go out of the window. Starting sentences with 'And' is common while using as few commas as possible is a requisite. You need to learn the subtleties of newspaper copy or face your work being hacked to pieces by a sub-editor and risk making an enemy on the sports desk.

Make your first port of call your local newsagents where you should pick up a handful of newspapers you want to write for. There are four types to consider:

- the broadsheets
- red top tabloids
- middle market tabloids
- regional press.

The broadsheets

The broadsheets have their own distinct style, so try reading *The Times*, *Telegraph* or *Guardian* for a feel of how their copy scans. There will inevitably be several words thrown in that will leave you scampering for your dictionary, but aside from that, take notice of the way the writer is given space to expand an idea. Whereas in a tabloid the writers need to be tight and get their points across within two sharp sentences at the most, broadsheets allow you the luxury of working in your own thoughts in depth.

Red tops

The red tops, like *The Sun* and *The Mirror*, are often cricitised for dumming down issues, but look carefully at the writing style – it is an art in itself. Trying to express an idea in a matter of words rather than sentences is extremely hard to do and the ability to turn a good phrase in a tight way will stand you in good stead in this market. Look at the intros as well, as they will either be hard-nosed or gimmicky in a bid to grab a reader's attention. This is where you need a good news sense or a bright imagination to ensure your piece is remembered above all others, but it will be hard because the competition is very strong.

Middle market

The middle market papers are generally classified as the *Daily Mail* and *Daily Express* and are slightly less extrovert in their approach, but that doesn't mean they want anything less than the same quality in their stories. In recent years the *Mail* has taken a harder edge and is keen for tales packed with controversy. The approach has worked as sales have boomed.

Regional papers

A regional paper is a title that comes out on a daily basis but looks at news only in its local area. They tend to follow the style set by the *Mail* and *Express* in their writing. They want to tell a story as it is without the glam and glitter provided by some of the national papers. But they are not afraid to pick up on important issues and campaign for change when necessary, even if that does mean demanding the head of the local football club chairman.

LEARNING A STYLE

Once you've bought your papers, sit down in your comfy chair with your feet up and read every word in them twice. Look at how the sentences are structured and the choice of word the journalist uses. Then pick any topic and write a 150-word piece using the same style of each newspaper. Do this every day for a week and you will soon find that it starts to come naturally to you. It is important to be comfortable with switching styles because it will be very useful as you progress. If you hit the top of the trade you will find yourself at a match writing for several publications at the same time and each title will demand that the copy fits their paper's style.

Improving your writing

An effective way to improve your writing is to set up a rota of things to write about. Since you plan to become a sports journalist, it's good to get the feel of writing about games early on, but do not just stick to sports as the experience of writing about different fields will keep your writing fresh. Try setting up a rota where you write a piece about the following each day:

- tape matches from TV and write reports
- review TV programmes
- write a news story about your day
- rewrite a match report from a national paper.

'Champions keep trying until they get it right.'

Billie Jean King

Joining a writing group

Writing groups are useful because they give you a showcase for your work and allow you the opportunity to gain feedback. Don't expect it to be a major step on the road to sports writing, though, as most people in the group are interested in writing short stories and poetry. Use the group to air some of your review work and listen to the advice – your fellow writers may not be experts, but it doesn't take an expert to spot a major problem with your writing.

Learning from home

Learning from home can be a great idea if you can afford it and can find the right course. Look for one that concentrates on getting news or sports stories published, as more general courses may take you too far away from what you want to do and you will lose interest. They do have many advantages and will:

- encourage you to write

- hone your skills

- allow you to receive individual feedback

- have a chance of earning back your outlay

- instil discipline in your work.

GETTING HELP FROM YOUR LOCAL TEC

If you plan to make a career out of freelance journalism and intend to set up your own company, contact your local Training and Enterprise Council for help and advice. Many TECs run courses for people starting up their own business and completion of one can lead to a financial award to help during your first weeks of self-employment.

The TEC is also useful as a reference point for any future business problems you come across. I contacted my local TEC before launching my own company called Presspass and was offered some valuable advice. Some also run an excellent monthly clinic where you can discuss problems with business experts free of charge.

CASE STUDIES

Andy is on course

After speaking to his careers teacher, Andy learns about the NCTJ course. Armed with a grant, he signs up for an eight-month stint at his local college hoping to land a job on a regional paper once he gets his qualifications. But while he enjoys the writing aspects, he finds the law and government lectures rather dull and struggles to pass his exams.

Jane teaches herself

As an English teacher, Jane is confident she does not need to undergo intensive training and decides to skip a course and learn newspaper style on her own. She buys a selection of papers each day and dissects them to discover how the articles are put together. Although she is disciplined enough to write every day, Jane finds it hard to throw out of the window the principles she teaches on a daily basis in order to fit into a tabloid style of writing.

CHECKLIST

1. Are you the right age for an NCTJ training course?

2. Have you phoned the contact numbers listed for more information?

3. Do restrictions on your time mean you should opt for a distance learning course?

4. Do you have the time to practise if you train yourself?

5. Have you read, and written in their style, a 150-word piece for every paper?

6. Are you writing match reports and TV reviews on a regular basis?

3

Buying the Right Equipment

BUYING THE BASICS

Freelance journalism is a wonderful area to move into because, unlike many other businesses or hobbies, the start-up costs are so small. Forget about having to fork out a fortune for all the latest pieces of kit that within two months will lay forgotten in your loft collecting dust. In journalism the most important factor is your ability to write – the tools you use to get your message across are secondary.

You can cover any sport with these three basic pieces of equipment:

1. a pen
2. a notepad
3. a stopwatch.

Access to a phone is also essential, but most of the sports you cover in your early days will be played in a public arena where a pay phone is usually accessible – negating the need for a mobile phone. If you are happy simply covering one or two games a week for your local paper, you need read no further. Just pop out to your local stationers and head to the nearest sports venue. If, though, you want to make a few pennies from sports writing, there are a few more things to buy.

BUYING A MOBILE PHONE

Annoying as they are, the mobile is a must for anybody keen to be taken seriously in this field. If you are at a big event and copy needs to be filed urgently, it is useless believing you can trundle to the nearest pay phone and wait for it to become free before placing your call to copy. You may even have to file copy as the event is proceeding, making darting off to find a phone impossible. Just think how much easier it is to pick up a phone in the comfort of your seat and file copy while your eyes are still glued on the action. Then there is no need to rush your words and risk mistakes in a desperate hurry to race back to your seat, and you won't miss out as Alan Shearer peels away to celebrate the goal of the season. But before buying a mobile phone think about the following:

- Are freephone numbers free so you can contact the national papers' copy departments without paying a charge?

- Will the reception be good enough when tucked away in a press box?

- Is the tariff long enough to avoid paying for too many peak-rate calls?

- How much does it cost to pick up your messages?

If you fail to research the answers to the above questions, you may end up paying far more than you need to keep your phone on the road, because once you are tied into a contract it is hard to get out for at least a year.

Another idea to look at is the rather clever offers set up to attract occasional callers, where you buy your 'air time' in advance and use up your tokens as you go along – paying for more calls as and when you need it. Under this contract you no longer have to pay a monthly sum to keep your phone alive. This set-up may be advantageous if you only plan to use your phone at sports events.

GETTING THE PERFECT COMPUTER SYSTEM

It is easy to spend a lifetime looking for the best deal on a computer, but to be honest it is not worth it as whatever you buy and wherever you do it, the next day there will be something bigger, better and cheaper on the market. But don't just jump at the first tasty offer you spot. Before buying there are a few things to consider, such as what you want to do on your computer. Do you want to:

- simply write sports stories – see **A**

- play games – see **B**

- organise your accounts – see **C**

- surf the internet – see **D**

A – If you just want a piece of kit to write your stories on, then look for a very basic machine. It needs to be able to handle a word processing package and if you want to send stories to newspapers via the telephone line, it also needs to include a modem.

B – So you want to be able to play a few games as well – who can blame you. Sometimes if you are struggling for the right word or come up against writer's block, it can be good to do something else for a short while. To play the latest games you need a machine with a fast Pentium-type processor and a CD-ROM to enjoy the best packages. These types of computers are getting incredibly cheap now so look around for bargains before buying.

C – It is best to find the accounting software you prefer before buying the machine (see Chapter 12) but it is handy to have a quick processor to make your number crunching easier.

D – Logging on has many advantages for freelance writers as you will find later on in this book. To ensure you can make the most of the wonderful world of the internet you need a quick processor with a system that has plenty of memory plus a fast modem.

Finding a travel companion

The more games you cover and more work you pick up, the more you will think about joining the growing group of journalists turning up at events showing off a laptop. Some laptops now are so powerful that you use them as your main home computer and then unplug a few wires and take them to the big match. But if you don't want to spend so much, look for a second-hand piece of kit in the computer magazines and at local computer fairs. As a minimum you will need to find a laptop that has a modem and enough space to load Windows 3.11 and a word processing package like Microsoft Works. Don't forget you will also need to buy the software and I would suggest a computer fair as the cheapest place to start looking. You can find the nearest one to you by looking in your local paper or checking the classified ads in a trade magazine. Once you are set up, the next step is to open a Newslink account – more of which later in this chapter.

FAXING FOR FUN

Times they are a-changing for the fax machine in the modern office, with most of the changes being for the worse if you are a fax lover. Once a necessity for any freelance operator, the arrival of the internet and email is starting to curtail the need for our clever friend. Busy newspapers and magazine editors do not want to be faced with the hassle of having to type up your script when it lands on their desk. As I will describe later, email and the Newslink system has ensured this is not necessary any more. But it is still a piece of kit worth having at the moment as the world has not yet clicked over into fully automated office life.

Which type of fax should you buy?
There are three options to look at.

1. Computer-based fax machines
Forget the need for endless streams of paper cluttering up your office. With a fax software package like WinFax or one of its rivals you can communicate using just your computer. Not only does this save printing out letters and having to put them through a fax machine, it is a great help if you want to save money on paper and keep your office tidy. These programs also save a lot of space in your office or home by cutting out the need for a stand-alone fax machine.

2. Fax machines
This is the type of fax you will be most used to and with the price for a small package dropping to just over the £100 mark they are indeed tempting to purchase. The biggest advantage over computer-based machines is the fact that you can send separate items like newspaper cuttings using this type of fax, whereas without a scanner you cannot do that with programs like Winfax.

3. The four-in-one machine
There is now also a third option to consider, one brought about by the amazing advances in modern technology – the all-singing, all-dancing fax/copier/scanner/printer. This marvel is an extremely useful tool and can run via your phone line along with your normal phone. It works in conjunction with your PC and provides the ability for you to complete various tasks without having your office overloaded with equipment. The more money you spend the better quality you enjoy, but at around £300 this excellent tool is worth investing in. Critics of the system claim there can be problems if one of the four components breaks down, and they are right because while it is being fixed you are left without the use of the other facilities.

LINKING UP WITH NEWSLINK

This is an excellent service and a must for anyone planning to set themselves up as a full-time freelance. Providing you have a modem, Newslink allows you to file copy to all of the UK's national newspapers, many regionals and the newsrooms of broadcast media. At the press of a button your story flies from your computer screen onto the copy-tasting system of numerous media outlets. You select where you want your story to go to and sit back and hope the copy is tempting enough to urge a newspaper to use it.

Newslink also keeps an archive of your story for seven years and in that time can tell you when and where it was sent to.

Best of all the system is free to subscribe to and it costs only 30 pence to send a story. For more information on setting up a Newslink account contact Cable & Wireless on 0500 190 400

SURFING THE INTERNET

The comedian Ben Elton once joked that the internet was full of amazing facts and figures – just like you find in a book at a library.

He was right, but the advantage of the internet is that this library takes up a very small space on your desk and there is no travelling involved.

To get started you need a computer with a modem. Then sign up with one of the many internet service providers (ISPs), who range from the computer giants like Microsoft to superstore giants Tesco. Most ISPs charge a monthly fee for the service but electrical goods group Dixons are promoting their own product called Freeserve, which as the name suggests costs nothing and provides a good service. Once you have selected your ISP and go on-line you can access millions of pages of information just by entering the odd word and clicking on your mouse.

The net – fabulous or frustrating?

Unfortunately the one thing that makes the internet so useful also makes it so annoying. There are millions of pages of information on the system and the sheer size of the tool causes problems for the search engines, which guide you to the information you are looking for. Typing in a common word can bring up thousands of matches and leave you pulling your hair out trying to find the exact topic you are after. To make life easier I suggest jotting down the address of any sites you think may be interesting when you spot them in newspapers and magazines and when you are surfing the web, bookmark sites you think may be useful in future.

Making your mark

Bookmarking allows you to find the website again by clicking on its name in a list of favourites you compile as you surf round the net. Once you tell the computer you want that site it does all the searching for you. Most internet providers have either a bookmark or favourite icon at the top of the page and when you click on this you will be asked if you want to add the current site on your screen to your favourites. By clicking yes it will be logged and ready to use next time you need it.

Five reasons to use the internet

- To find information about your sport in different areas of the world.

- To read the latest output from major news organisations.

- To keep up to date with a sports club via their webpage.

- To find background information before an interview.

- To hear radio broadcasts via the net.

USING EMAIL

This wizard of a system is one of the wonders of modern science and not as hard to operate as you may think. Email is a message sent between two computers via a modem. Once you have the software installed (it usually comes with your ISP), you are greeted with a box and you insert an address and then your message. The beauty of email is the attachment facility that allows you to write you story in a standard word processor file and simply tack it onto the email. The recipient then opens the file and can work with the text. You can also cut and paste any work straight from your word processor into the message box. Do this by highlighting the text you want to send and use the cut command from your word processor's tool bar. Then switch to your message box and click on the pasteboard icon and the text will appear. If this all sounds a bit tricky, there are plenty of books on the market to help you out.

GETTING IT ALL ON TAPE

Dictaphones comes in many shapes and sizes these days but they are still as important as ever. No matter how quick your shorthand is, there will be people you interview who speak faster than you can write, so it is worth investing in a Dictaphone. They are also a help when you are doing long interviews, as they give you a chance to think ahead about questions rather than simply concentrating on getting the quotes down correctly.

SENDING WORDS VIA DATA SUITES AND PCMICA CARDS

Although pricey, a Data Suite or a PCMICA card could make a major difference to your freelance career if you intend to take it seriously. Each piece of equipment allows journalists to file copy from their laptops using only a mobile phone. So even if you are stuck in the middle of nowhere you can send your story as soon as you find out about it. Just think, you could be driving to a friend's house when you get a vital phone call with some quotes that are perfect for a certain publication, but you need to send them quickly to ensure you beat your rivals to the punch. With a Data Suite or PCMICA card, a mobile phone and an account with Newslink, you just have to park up, type the story, set up the necessary kit and the job is done there and then.

TAKING THE WEIGHT OFF YOUR FINGERS

If you have a Pentium chip computer you can now buy software that allows you to talk to your machine rather than type. If you are a bad typist this package, that can cost less than £50, could be a godsend and save you from many tears of frustration, but if you can type you may not need it. While the thought of easing back into your favourite chair and putting your feet up while chatting to your computer may sound relaxing, it will not work as quickly or as accurately as the kit God has already given you – your ten fingers.

A LITTLE KNOWLEDGE GOES A LONG WAY

You can arm yourself to the teeth with all the electronic gadgets and hi-tech tools you need, but without a bit of knowledge you will never make a penny. Newspapers have little desire to speak to you just because you have a nice writing style or a fancy computer. They will order tales from you because you have a bit of knowledge no one else has given them. From the announcement of star speaker at a local rugby club dinner to the latest signing at the town's football club, it is the knowledge they are after.

How to build up knowledge
There are two areas to develop, the first being your contacts in the field, which we will discuss later in the book. The other is background knowledge to give your stories more credibility. Most sports have their own reference books (for football it is the *Rothmans Yearbook* that is the most popular), but don't forget to look beyond the obvious. Your local cricket club may have a centenary yearbook or the squash club may have a monthly newsletter packed full of facts that can make you sound like an expert.

Pick up as much information as you can because you never know when you may need it. Sporting almanacs are useful and anything with lists of results is worth keeping hold of. Get in touch with the governing body of the sport you are planning to cover as they may issue a newsletter and put you on their mailing list. Read newspapers every day and listen to radio broadcasts to make sure you are up to date with all your facts. And of course there is always the internet for a whole plethora of information.

Do not retire the old favourites
In your rush to get your hands on the latest computer do not forget a couple of old friends who can prove vital in a crisis – the dictionary and Thesaurus . . .

CASE STUDIES

Andy gets lucky on the lottery
A small win on the lottery hands Andy some spare cash and keen not to waste it he invests in the future by buying a laptop and a mobile phone. He finds the freedom the laptop gives him helps improve his writing when covering live events as he can see his words and change them on screen quickly and effortlessly. Now all he needs is a chance to put his practice runs into action.

Jane splashes out
Jane decides to plunder her savings so she can afford to buy a new home computer. Her husband is keen to get on the internet so they buy a machine with a high level processor and a modem. She also

buys a computer fax package so she can fax her stories to a newspaper in the future.

CHECKLIST

1. Have you bought a reliable stopwatch?

2. Do you really need to buy that mobile phone?

3. Have you checked which dealer gives you freephone calls free of charge?

4. What components does your computer need if you want to use the internet?

5. Can your computer host a fax package to save you buying a fax machine?

6. Who has the best ISP package according to a trade magazine?

7. Is your email account up and running?

4

Researching the Market Place

Unlike many other trades, the writing market is small and very insular. Despite the fact that your newsagent has shelves full of magazines, there are not endless customers for you to approach. What you see is all there is and there can be very few trades where the customer base is so scant. But do not be disheartened as every one of those magazines and newspapers needs new and original stories and if you can provide them on a regular basis they will keep coming back for more. There are too many titles for me to go through each one individually, but in this chapter I will delve into the different areas of the market you should be looking at writing for.

WRITING FOR THE LOCAL PRESS

This is your starting point as there are plenty of weekly and daily regional papers you can target – from the advert-filled freebie that comes through your letterbox once a week to the local daily paper that covers your patch. Some of the bigger regional papers even produce specialised sports papers on a Saturday filled with opportunities for a freelance.

But before you get straight on the phone to the sports editor to tell them about the brilliant stories you are going to write for them, first study the paper and every sports story it contains. Look at what type of sports get better coverage and which ones rarely merit a mention. Which leagues have big spreads and which ones are glossed over with one or two paragraphs? Write all this information down and then ask why? Does the lack of coverage mean the paper has no reliable correspondent for that sport and hence here lies an opportunity for you? Or is that sport simply not very popular in the region? Reasons for sparse coverage of a sport include:

- a lack of space in the paper

- not enough people interested in it

- sports editor is not a fan

- no one is providing decent coverage.

If the last option is the reason, there is an opportunity for you, so get on the phone to the sports desk and ask if you can help out. But do not approach the desk in an aggressive manner or you will find you get short shrift for your efforts. Phoning up and fuming about the fact that there is not enough ice-hockey coverage in the paper is not the way to pick up work. Try a different approach, like asking whether the ice-hockey stories are not very prominent because the paper is not being supplied with enough tales. If this is the case, volunteer your services. We will look at how to do that in the next chapter.

WHO SHOULD YOU SPEAK TO ON A SPORTS DESK?

At this point it is worthwhile explaining how a regional paper sports desk works to help you understand the chain of command.

Weekly papers
Here you will find sports editors are generally jacks of all trades and tend to work on their own. They can write about any sport and design page layouts at the same time. They may also do subbing work, which includes rearranging your copy if they are not happy with it.

Regional papers
On bigger regionals, the desk is run by the sports editor who decides the content and also designs pages. He will have a deputy who takes over the reins when his boss is off but is reluctant to make decisions without referring to the sports editor first. If there are local rugby, football or cricket teams that play at a high standard, there will generally be a reporter for each. These journalists will also cover one or two of the minority sports.

Freelancers
In both weekly and regional papers, the reporters will cover their main team, but the copy that fills up the majority of the space tends to come from an outside source. Cricket, football and rugby leagues will each have a secretary who writes a weekly round-up. Local sports clubs will have an officer who files regular copy on his outfit. There will also be some sports covered by people just like you – who want to make extra money from their combined joys of writing and sport.

Sub-editors
Before a piece finds its way onto the page, it is checked by a sub who corrects anything he or she feels is wrong. This quite often means

changing sentences and leaving you looking silly by either deleting a vital fact or ruining the structure of your piece. Unfortunately as a freelance these are problems you have to live with. Once you hand your copy over, it is up to the paper what it wants to do with it.

EXPLORING THE MAGAZINE MARKET

When I was young there were only two sports magazines to read – *Shoot* and *Match* – both of them aimed at the teenage football market. How times have changed. In recent years as the game has grown, a plethora of magazines have hit the newsagents shelves with front cover pictures of Ryan Giggs and Michael Owen tempting football fanatics to take them to the cash tills. This explosion has not just been good for football writers, though, as the success of soccer magazines has rubbed off on other sports titles. Several multi-sport publications have started and even specialist titles aimed at rugby and cricket are back in favour.

UNDERSTANDING THE ROLE OF AGENCIES

There are two types of agency in the media world and both can prove helpful to you in your bid to fulfil your dream of making money from your hobby:

* the large multinational organisation that supplies a wire service to papers

* the local press agency that provides freelance copy to other media outlets.

Both provide opportunities for you to sell your work, but we will start by looking at the big boys.

The Press Association

When it comes to sport reporting in Britain, PA sets the industry standard for a whole host of activities. If you are an editor and want to know the time of the first goal at Anfield, the first horse past the post at Goodwood or Tim Henman's third-round opponent at Wimbledon, the Press Association is where you turn to. They provide the official line for every major sport in this country and their contacts with foreign agencies help them provide worldwide coverage as well. Every sports desk in the country from the nationals to your local paper has a PA feed in their office and refers to it constantly. Even sports stars know all about the benefits of using PA. When former Southampton manager Graeme Souness left the club he issued a statement to stop papers sending staff reporters chasing him around the world and of course it was sent to PA.

How to benefit

The nature of the beast leaves PA keen to find and report stories on all sports from across Britain. It is wonderful news for freelancers as it gives you an opportunity to sell your sports tales. But make contact with the sports desk first and ensure they are interested in what you have to offer and do not already have someone looking after the event in question.

Martin's advice

Assistant sports editor Martin Zeigler reveals it is important for the fledgling freelancer to realise that the smaller the club the better the story has to be:

'We are after stories with strong news angles rather than just a good piece of writing. Stories about signings, or a prominent person at a club saying something new and worthwhile are always of interest to us. Obviously the bigger the club or the name the less strong the story has to be, whereas with smaller clubs the story has to be a lot stronger. We do not want stories from local golf or squash tournaments. We take results but that is all and they are supplied by regular contacts.'

PA can receive copy by phone, fax, email and via the Newslink service mentioned earlier, but Zeigler stresses it is not worth filing unless the news desk have shown an interest in the story.

When speaking to the desk Zeigler feels it is important to make a good immediate impression:

'You can do that by being professional and enthusiastic. Know what you are talking about and show you understand what makes a good story. It is also important that people are not put off by a knockback when they offer a story for the first time. They need to keep coming back with stories whenever they find them if they want to become regular contributors to us.'

Reuters

Reuters is a slightly different kettle of fish to PA as they provide a worldwide service supplying companies like the Press Association in hundreds of countries with the latest sporting news from across the globe. They are not too interested in getting involved in the nuts and bolts of British sport. For example, they will take a story about Manchester United's latest £10 million signing, but will not be interested in Crewe's latest free transfer. They tend to have a web of qualified journalists covering Britain and are therefore not too keen on phone calls asking if they need events covered.

But if you have struck lucky and managed to set up an interview with a recognised world star, give them a call.

Local agencies

Across Britain there is a network of freelance sports reporters running press agencies. I even run one myself called Presspass, which is based in Manchester and like many others it supplies copy to the national papers and just about everyone else featured in this chapter. Because of their size, they will be reluctant to take anyone on full-time, but an offer to help out on matchdays may prove to be a godsend to them. Personally I would not use anyone for my agency who has not had newspaper experience, but I am just one of a hundred so do not be put off contacting local agencies. The best way to find your nearest one is to contact the sports editor on your local paper and ask him if he can help point you in the right direction.

LOGGING INTO THE MULTIMEDIA REVOLUTION

The arrival of the internet heralds all kinds of promises of work for the freelance journalist, but at the moment the jury is still very much out on whether that will ever be the case. The medium has yet to find its feet despite several attempts to paceset by various media groups. Most of the sports content on the websites is taken directly from the PA and Reuters wire and put out verbatim. Several national and regional papers have their own sites, but again they only use content taken from their publication.

There are a few sites trying to buck the trend like Football 365, which aims to provide an original service, and the English Cricket Board's excellent service which is edited by Julian Goode.

Julian's advice

Julian runs the Lord's website and he believes the scope for freelancers planning to sell work to internet-based publications could blossom once the market starts to grow.

'It is a great opportunity for the MCC to get their message across directly to cricket lovers. Without this site the only real contact they have with cricket fans is when people book tickets or make a point of writing to them.

I think this area is one that is growing and growing and will open up new markets for freelance writers in time. The one problem is probably finding out which websites are interested in taking freelance work. But it is like any market – you have to do your research. If you were selling to magazines you would go into newsagents and look at what is on the shelves. If you want to sell to people on the internet you need to get on-line and see what sites there are in the areas you want to work in.

But the potential is enormous as the freelancer at his computer in St John's Wood no longer only has his local paper and a few magazines to aim at. From his seat in front of the computer he could be selling his work to websites that originate from all over the world.'

Opening your own website

You could always start your very own website revolution. Several companies offer free homepages for you to use providing you advertise their products and with a few more ads and a lot of visitors, who knows, you could strike gold. But that is highly doubtful unless you can come up with an idea no one has thought of yet. To be honest this is an area that has to be watched as it has yet to find its home in the media world.

Julian Goode, however, believes the internet is definitely an area of attack for the freelance:

'In Britain we have only been on-line for five years whereas newspapers have been going for two centuries, so it won't happen overnight. But the publishing business is all about advertising and if you can produce a product that will attract people to a site then the advertisers will follow. I have no doubt this is a growing market and there will be a lot of money involved in the internet.'

LOOKING ABROAD TO MAKE SOME BUCKS

A few years ago selling to foreign markets was unthinkable because the cost of giving copy and chasing accounts of papers and magazines in foreign countries was prohibitive. The major publications who use copy from Britain had their own correspondents making the need to buy from a freelance unnecessary. But with the advent of the internet, email and cheaper home computers, there are endless opportunities.

Cashing in on foreign sales

A friend of mine went to America to cover the Atlanta Olympics in 1996 and contacted a few papers before he went, offering coverage of an athlete from their particular area. The idea took off and he was inundated with orders, not just from Britain but across the world. Now he lives in the States and has set up a thriving freelance business using the money he made from the Olympics as his start-up capital.

Obviously you don't want to wait until the next Olympics to cash in but there are plenty of opportunities already in this country. Why not approach the hometown paper of a foreign rugby league player, who is starring for your local league team, and offer them interviews and snippets about his progress in this country. There are plenty of sports and plenty of foreign competitors and they will be willing to speak to you if they know the piece is for their hometown paper. Of course, if English is your only language you are restricted a bit to America and the Commonwealth countries, but if you are bi-lingual the world's your oyster.

CASE STUDIES

No job joy for Andy

After getting an adequate grade on his course, Andy finds it hard to pick up a job on a local newspaper. He also realises that it will be several years before he moves on to a sports desk even if he does find a decent job. He decides to look at the freelance market and goes into his newsagent and buys every title he feels he could work for to find out exactly what the market place is like.

Magazines are OK for Jane

Jane finds it too hard to adapt to the tabloid style at the moment and plans to concentrate on the magazine market. A trip to the newsagents reveals very few titles on her favourite sports so she contacts the Sports Council (see addresses), who give her a listing of all the bodies in charge of the activities she likes. She phones them up and is given numbers for several titles she would be unable to find in high street shops. After subscribing she starts to devour the content of each magazine and thinks about making her mark.

CHECKLIST

1. Does your local paper have any areas you can cover?

2. What is the role of a sub-editor?

3. What does a local freelance agency do?

4. Which stories will PA take from a freelancer?

5. What is the best way to discover the internet market place?

5

Talking to Sports Editors

MAKING THE FIRST CONTACT

When you start out on this long and hopefully profitable road, the local paper's sports editor is the most important person in the world to you. If you can get their ear and convince them you are a writer worth dealing with, they will help you take a big step on the way to achieving your dreams. Therefore your first contact is vitally important and you have to make the right impression.

Unfortunately sports editors these days are under tremendous pressure because of cost-cutting exercises at most papers. This can work in your favour as it means more copy has to be produced by freelancers and this is where you can be a help to the sports editor. But because of the pressure, the modern sports editor is a busy person and arriving at the newspaper's office at 9 am on a Monday morning demanding a meeting is not the best approach.

Knowing the right time to call

Although most regional papers are delivered to our doors in the evening, the majority of the hard work that goes into producing them takes place in the morning. So do not even think about making an introductory phone call before 11am as even the best prepared script in the world is not going to make an impression.

When you do get hold of the sports editor do not expect to be invited down for lunch at the paper's expense or you will be in for a major let down. And do not try to be their best friend by offering to buy them lunch in the nearest pub. It's a Catch-22 situation as until the sports editor has met you they will view you as a time-consuming nuisance, so the thought of spending their precious lunch hour with you is not appetising.

The best approach is to ask whether the sports editor would be willing to see some of your work. At this point you may not have had anything printed but send in a few typewritten stories you feel are your most accomplished pieces. Follow this up with a phone call and volunteer to visit the office for a five-minute chat at their convenience.

Making the right impression

Here are a few things to remember for when you do finally meet up:

- Be polite and friendly.

- Take your cuttings with you.

- If you have no cuttings take typed copies of your work.

- Ask in which areas the sports editor lacks cover.

- Offer to specialise in that area.

- Also offer to cover the sport you are most interested in.

- Be prepared to take on tasks you may not fancy the idea of.

- Ask who the number two on the desk is so you have more than one contact.

It is important to make a good impression because when you supply copy to their paper you are representing the publication and the last thing the sports editor wants is the potential for complaints about you. During my spell in regional papers there was a young buck desperate to earn an opportunity on the sports desk and he was lucky to be given a chance to write a few pieces. But within a month he had upset the manager of one of the local football teams and was spotted by the deputy editor being thrown out of a sports event. He compounded his predicament by hurling abuse at the organisers claiming the paper would write a bad report on the incident. Needless to say he was not used again.

Chris's advice

Chris Harvey was an experienced sports editor before being promoted to the role of Production Editor on the *Hull Daily Mail*. He believes a softly, softly approach when trying to contact sports editors has more chance of working than battering down the door.

'The best way is to ring in, to be honest. It doesn't really work with letters. At least with a phone call you will get an honest answer and you can do it in two minutes rather than waste time composing a letter. In a phone call you can put them in the picture and a sports editor can tell you there and then whether they use freelancers. If you think from the phone call you are being fobbed off, send in a business card asking for it to be put in the contacts book.'

It is best to explain everything you are capable of doing for the sports desk in the initial call rather than just one particular game you fancy covering. Chris adds:

'Whether you get a favourable response from the call depends on circumstances. If you have all sorts of skills to offer just come clean. If you are willing to cover most sports tell them as well as explaining what you have done so far. Although you have to impress the sports editor it is good to remember that sometimes we need you as much as you need the work.'

But Chris is adamant that bowling up on a Monday morning demanding a meeting will earn you few brownie points.

'That is the worst thing you can do. Wait until the sports editor volunteers it before even thinking about meeting.'

Keeping in their good books

After the first meeting ensure any work you agree to undertake is delivered on time, is accurate and is well written. If it isn't there is no point speaking to the sports editor again. Unfortunately you may not be asked to do any work following the first meeting and if that is the case it's time for you to find a few stories. It's during this period that you can start to build up a relationship by keeping in contact with the sports editor. *But*:

Don't ring every day.
Do write with a list of ideas.
Don't complain about lack of opportunities.
Do phone if you pick up a good tale.
Don't moan about stories in the paper.
Do let the editor know if you are attending a match or event.

How do you know when the relationship is in place?

* When you can ring and do not have to explain who you are.

* When the sports editor returns your call.

* When you are asked to cover an event.

* When other members of the desk are helpful.

More advice from Chris

Chris Harvey believes that once the all-important first meeting is out of the way you should avoid bombarding the desk with phone calls pleading for work.

'Once you've made the initial contact I think there is no harm in ringing up once more to ask if the sports editor has thought any more about using you. You should be able to feel whether you are getting the brush off or whether when the sports editor says there is nothing at the moment, he means it. Once you have made this call, though, leave it or you will risk becoming a pest.'

If things go to plan and you can provide the quality of work you have promised, Chris believes it is easy to build up a good relationship. He adds:

'You will know when you have a good relationship in place when the sports editor makes the approach to you and asks if you can do a job for him. When that happens you can start ringing up regularly and offering your services.'

Asking for work

Once you have built up a decent relationship asking for work becomes easy and has a natural feel to it. If you are at an event it is a case of telling the sports editor which star is there or who is playing and adding at the end 'would you like any copy?'

Or if you have a tale, describe the premise and ask 'would you like me to file a piece on it?' Sounds easy, doesn't it? Well, it can be if you sell the idea correctly.

Here are some ways to increase your chances of making an editor say 'yes'.

- Don't just say 'I'm going to a game'. Tell them what makes this game the best of the weekend.

- Don't pick games they already have staff at; for example, a Premiership football match.

- Do mention the names of any big sports stars who will be there.

- Explain why the occasion is important to the community.

MAKING CONTACT WITH NATIONAL SPORTS DESKS

In every person's heart there is a dream and anyone with a desire to do well in their chosen field has to have something to aim for. But if your flight of fancy is built around picking up a phone on your first day of being a sports writer and convincing an editor on a broadsheet title that you are the perfect person to pen a piece on the England cricket captain, it's time you had a reality check. Achieving your goal will be a long hard slog which may never bear fruit and instead feed you a dish of rotten apples. Although I would never knock ambition, I would suggest you start on the regional papers and first learn your trade then move up the scale – how quickly you do is up to you.

First contact

Write to the sports editor and wait a week to make sure the letter has been received and read. You will never actually speak to this exalted being, so do not be disgruntled that when you place your follow-up call you are told the letter has been passed to the sports news editor. Now it is time to track down the person who will be your main contact if you are lucky enough to break into this field. Unlike local papers, the best time to reach the sports news editor is late morning and undoubtedly your first call will be a brief uninterested conversation where you are told there are no openings at the moment.

At this point all your plans could be thrown into turmoil unless you hold your nerve and have a little trick up your sleeve. I would suggest only calling when you have a national event of a minority sport occurring within travelling distance from you. So when the sports news editor tries to give you the brush off, nip in and ask if they object to your filing a few paras on the event you have selected. Then get off the phone with either a heavy heart or a skip in your step.

The next stage

If the answer was 'yes' then look forward to a day worth writing about in your diary. If they said 'no' do not be too down-hearted. Keep your eyes and ears peeled for similar events to the one you promised to cover. If you can't find them right away don't worry, the under-pressure news editor will have already forgotten your conversation. Now it is time for the hard slog, visit these events, file copy on the numbers printed later in the chapter and keep hoping to see your piece in the paper.

Mike's advice

Daily Express sports editor Mike Allen warns freelancers not to attempt contacting national papers until they have plenty of writing experience and a strong cuttings file behind them:

'If you have never written for newspapers before you will be found out very quickly. And once your name has been tarred it will be very hard to earn the chance to prove yourself again. We are looking for people who have good experience of writing for papers and are looking for a chance to work on a bigger stage.'

But Mike suggests that if your writing is up to scratch getting a break in national papers can be more about good fortune than ability:

'It can be down to luck. We might have a vacancy or a redundancy, which means we need a freelance to cover a certain area. If a freelance phones up at that moment they could get the work above someone who may be a better writer simply because they phoned at the right time.'

Like Chris Harvey, Mike believes a phone call is the best way to make your first approach:

'Put in a phone call and follow it up with a letter explaining a bit about yourself and what you can do. But once you have done that, don't phone up every day and ask for work as it will only antagonise the desk.'

Once you are in print

Now is the time to phone back the news editor and explain that your piece was used and offer to cover another small-scale event on your patch. If they give you the go ahead you have started what could be a promising relationship. If they say 'no', it's back to the hard slog.

A relationship is built

After seeing your name in print a few times it is worth stepping up the campaign. In every sport there are a number of games taking place on a regular basis, the most high profile of these sports being football. And for every match each paper devises a match-list where they instruct regular freelancers to go to games for them and provide copy. Now is the time to aim for the match-list, although expect a struggle as this is hallowed ground. Just mention you would be free to cover a lower-scale professional game on your patch and hope for a positive response. You may well be told the paper does not need any more help just now, but do not give up. Wait for another low-key event to arrive and try again.

More advice from Mike

Once you have made an initial contact, Mike believes there are two ways to keep your services in the spotlight:

'If you have a firm story, contact the desk and ask them if they would be interested in taking the piece. Or file your stories with no prerequisite to copy and if it is used you will be paid. The more stories we see that are useful to the paper the more chance there is of the freelancer being contacted for work. It can also help if you know someone on the paper's staff. If they sound out the sports editor and tell them a call is coming it can help pave the way. It will give you more credibility if you have been recommended and make the sports editor more inclined to listen.'

Ensuring repeat custom

There is one way and one way only to make sure you work for the publication again – do a good job. If you can produce an article with no mistakes that needs no correction before it goes in the paper, the next time you ring offering to provide your services the sports editor will be inclined to say 'yes'. And if you manage to write a piece that is outstanding and in doing so have picked up some quotes from a star name whom the sports editor never expected you to approach, then he will start ringing you to give you work.

If you get names, times and scores wrong plus you slander a well-known sports celebrity in the process, change your phone number.

Asking how much you will be paid

'Pirmin does not ski for money or to be famous. He loves to ski and he wants to be perfect.'

Marc Biver, Pirmin Zurbriggen's manager

There is no need to feel nervous about this one as you will not be forced to indulge in a bartering match with sports editors. Most papers have standard rates and you will be paid accordingly. If you are money mad ask how much the job will pay and if you're not happy with the rate don't do the work. In fact don't bother ringing again as you lack the commitment to make a good fist of this game. Only when you are fully established can you start to hanker over cash. Initially just take the work and take whatever payment is on offer.

ENTERING A TRADITIONALLY MALE WORLD

Like sport itself, sports journalism is a rough tough world and the freelance market is the toughest of them all. Making a breakthrough is a long hard struggle and it is probably even more daunting if you are a female journalist. No matter how well you know your chosen sport, it will still be a battle to gain credibility with the players and your peers. There is no easy answer other than banging on as many doors as possible until one opens.

Janine's advice

Janine Self is now a football reporter on *The Sun* but she admits her freelance days were troublesome:

> 'I was slightly luckier than most as I had been at *The Mirror* and had a bit of a reputation, but I think any female freelance journalist will find it hard to get work. You have to know people. If you just ring up cold it will be difficult. It is hard enough for any freelance to ring up cold but for a woman it is virtually impossible.
>
> Although it may be hard with the desks, being a female journalist is probably an advantage when it comes to dealing with players and managers. They are actually quite old-fashioned and will not talk to women as brusquely as a guy. You obviously can't go out and drink 25 pints with a player but they tend to remember you more because you are a woman.
>
> I've only once had problems and that was with a certain football manager. I said watching his team was a dull experience and the next time he saw me he told me to stick to knitting. But that turned into a bit of a joke and we get on fine now. It probably helped build up the working relationship.'

CONTACTING MAGAZINE EDITORS

Unlike daily papers, which can take any story because it is fresh, magazines have a hard job in making sure they do not look dated when they hit the news stands. This job is doubly hard because the issue is put together several weeks before it hits the shelves. The fact that they have the space to print lengthy pieces is an advantage as it gives them a chance to expand on any issue that comes up during interview, and their willingness to look beyond the top level of the sport is an added bonus. So when targeting a magazine you will need to come up with an idea that will not date and will not be picked up by the papers in the meantime.

The features editor's dilemma

On magazines it is the features editor who commissions the work and it is important to them that they know the calibre of the people who are offering them work. They do not want to pick up the pieces for someone who makes a mess of a situation while claiming they are working for their publication. And they do not want to spend their days rewriting copy because the quality of work is so poor. That is why *Shoot*'s Luke Nicoli and every other features editor wants to see cuttings from past work before they commission you, as they are desperate to ensure the work they have ordered arrives without any hitches.

Their standpoint is fair enough. Imagine you are decorating your house and you order some undercoat paint. You expect it to arrive on time and be in a good enough condition to use because if it isn't you cannot add the top coat and finish the job. That is the same position a features editor is in if they order work from you that is not delivered to the appropriate standards on time. But whereas you could wait a week to paint the walls, the magazine has a deadline to be met or the publisher loses a small fortune. It is no surprise, therefore, that features editors are careful when you first contact them about work.

Luke's advice

Like other features editors, Luke Nicoli is willing to take good quality work from freelancers but will check out their credentials before agreeing to accept the articles:

'If people come on to me with a story or feature that is new and a little bit different to anything I have seen before, I will definitely be interested. But if I have never taken work from them before I will ask for their cuttings and make a few calls to ensure the work stands up.

If they claim to have arranged an interview with someone like Dennis Bergkamp I will check with his agent to find out if this is true. So they have to be honest and tell me exactly where the work is coming from.

We like to have question-and-answer style interviews with the game's top stars in *Shoot* and getting the big names is not easy. But if someone has managed to speak to a top name and their credentials stand up we will take their work even if they are a freelance.'

The credibility problem

It's a pity there isn't a shop in the high street that sells credibility. It would be a lot easier just to pop in there between buying milk and eggs and pick it up off the shelf rather than go through the years of hard work needed to gain credibility in the real world.

Unfortunately it is very much the chicken and egg situation to begin with and as you've probably guessed there are no easy solutions. The best way to get a foot in the door is to come up with an original idea that you can easily produce. It's no good promising a publication a feature with Ronaldo as, although they would love to have it, you will have to be very lucky to gain an interview with someone of his celebrity status.

Instead concentrate on the sports world around you. Maybe there is a budding badminton star in your area who is the daughter of a famous rugby player or a local team that has failed to win a game in two years. Once you've hit on an idea and confirmed you can come up with the goods, get on the phone and propose it to the features editor in a positive manner.

Being positive

There is no point getting a busy editor on the phone and then telling them shyly that you have an idea they probably will not want to use about someone they may not have heard of. Would you commission a feature on that premise? Talk up the idea by advising them how big a star this person is going to be and inform them why the idea will make people want to read the piece. Positive statements include:

- 'He's the next Michael Owen.'

- 'People in the area believe he will win a gold medal.'

- 'She's got a really interesting background.'

- 'I doubt you will have heard a story like this before.'

GETTING A TRACK RECORD

Once you've got your foot in the door, finding work will become a lot easier. A few years ago I became aware of the phrase 'money leads to money' and it is relevant in the sports-writing market as well. To put it a little less crudely, as we Brits hate to talk about something as brash as cash, you can translate it into 'work leads to work' – confused?

Well, it's simple – the more your name is in print the more work you will pick up. I write occasional pieces for *Total Football* after a chance meeting with their features editor Alex Murphy at a press conference. At the time he said there were no jobs for me in the near future, but soon after I managed to persuade him to let me interview Tim Flowers for the magazine. No doubt his decision may have been influenced by a rather large match report on Liverpool in the previous Sunday's *News of the World*. To spell it out for you, the more times your by-line is seen the more credibility you have.

CASE STUDIES

Andy gets a break
Confident his journalism training will open a few doors, Andy rings round his local papers and is invited to send in some of his work. Within a week he is asked to cover a non-league football game on his patch and told if he does a good job he can continue to write for the paper on a regular basis.

Hard work for Jane
Despite finding new markets, Jane finds it hard to spark any interest from the titles she writes to asking for work. The majority of them fail to reply and the ones who do extend that courtesy explain they already have enough freelancers on their books and do not require any more help. Frustrated by the response Jane considers giving up, but a talk with her husband helps her focus her thoughts and she decides to battle on.

CHECKLIST

1. Who is the most important person to you when you start out?

2. When is the best time to contact a sports editor on a regional paper?

3. How do you know when you have built up a relationship?

4. What is the best way to encourage an editor to say 'yes' to your ideas?

5. Is it a good idea to haggle over your payment?

6. What is the feature editor's dilemma?

7. Is there an easy way to get credibility?

8. Why will getting a track record be a help to you?

6

Making Contacts

IT'S WHO YOU KNOW ...

You can produce better prose than Dickens and have a keener eye for detail than a sniper, but without contacts you will never become a successful sports writer. Contacts are the lifeblood of any hopeful freelancer because they are the people who tell you what is going on before the rest of the world knows. And, of course, if you know what is going on first you are the person liable to make money out of the story. But how do you meet them and more importantly get them to tell you something that is worth a pretty penny? Simple. As Norman Tebbitt once said, 'get on your bike.'

Who is a contact:

A contact is anyone who can reliably tell you something you did not know. They can include:

- a sportsman or woman

- the manger or coach of a club

- press officers

- committee members

- fans in the know

- the landlord of the local pub.

Getting to know the press officers

A press officer is an important contact to have. They can talk to the top people at the club when you are unable to talk to them and supply you with information. A press officer can also give you 'guidance' on a matter the club does not want to be quoted on. If a club wants to make an announcement to the media it will come through the press office in the form of a press release (see Figure 1). But beware – sometimes clubs use press officers as a means to block you from finding out vital information by telling you to make all your enquiries

25.JUN.1998 15:36   EVERTON   NO.393   P.1/1

THE FOOTBALL CLUB COMPANY LIMITED

GOODISON PARK
LIVERPOOL L4 4EL
Tel. (Administration)
0151 330 2200
Fax 0151 286 9112
Tel. (Box Office)
0151 330 2300
Fax 0151 286 9119

PRESS RELEASE

HOWARD KENDALL LEAVES EVERTON FOOTBALL CLUB

Everton Football Club today announced that the contract of Team Manager Howard
Kendall had been terminated by mutual consent.

Speaking today, Chairman Peter Johnson said,

"Howard and I have sat down and following amicable discussions it was felt in the
long term interests of the Club that his contract be terminated. Obviously it saddens
me that this has happened, for Howard is a man of the highest integrity and cares
passionately for this Club. I am bitterly disappointed that his third term in office did
not end on a more successful note, but he will always receive a warm welcome at
Goodison Park, and our best wishes go with him for the future."

Howard Kendall commented,

"When I returned to Goodison Park nearly 12 months ago, I genuinely felt I had
returned to my footballing roots and fully expected to end my managerial career at the
Club where I had experienced so many triumphs, but it was not to be. I leave with
regrets, but I know our supporters will understand that a Club of this stature demands
success. I have no doubt that better times will eventually return, and to the best
supporters in the land I say a sincere thank you. Evertonians have always been and
will remain close to my heart."

The Club added that the post of Team Manager will be advertised and in the
meantime the Assistant Manager, Adrian Heath, will assume responsibilities for team
affairs.

Ends

25 June 1998

Secretary
M.J. DUNFORD
Manager
H. KENDALL

Registered Number
36624, England

Official Kit Supplier

Official Club Sponsor

UMBRO
Only Football

Fig. 1. Example of a press release.

through them. Don't fall into the lazy trap of putting a call into the press office and believing everything you are told. Sometimes you may need to dig a little.

FINDING YOUR CONTACTS

The most obvious place to find someone in the know is at a sporting occasion, but there is no point turning up expecting your target to drop everything to speak to you. Approaching them at half-time of a big match will not bring the results you are looking for. Wait until afterwards and catch them heading to the bar or their car and then introduce yourself, making sure you give them the following information:

- who you are
- who you write for
- the fact that you only want to speak for a minute
- the subject you want to talk to them about.

Do not be intimidated. Forget about star status; even the mega-rich high profile sports players are human just like you. If you ask a polite question they will generally be polite in return. And, of course, if you are rude you may not get the response you are looking for. So when you approach them just be natural and strike up a conversation about a topic relevant to them which is inoffensive. They will no doubt still have the game they have just played filling their mind so it is prudent to ask them about the match. Don't forget that to the sports star you are a stranger and asking them to tell you about the latest sex scandal in the changing room will draw a blank, and probably a rude one at that. Ensure the first contact is reasonably brief but that it gives you a platform to build on when you approach them the second time.

Simon's advice

The *Daily Star*'s Simon Mullock believes contacts are the lifeblood of any successful sports journalist and is convinced the first meeting is vital:

'When you see the person you want to speak to, simply introduce yourself and take the bull by the horns. But don't bulldoze in when they are talking to someone. Wait for them to finish whatever they are doing or you won't get the reaction you are looking for. First impressions are very important and if you don't show any kind of manners you are backing a loser from the start.'

Even once he has met the star, Mullock always ensures he re-introduces himself when he next wants to speak to them:

'Every time I see someone who is a contact I say 'hello' and tell them my name even if I'm not going to interview them there and then. It helps reaffirm who I am in their minds, because I can guarantee they will struggle to remember your name ten minutes after the first contact.'

Your number's up

Once you feel confident that the sportsman or woman is willing to chat to you on a regular basis, it is time to ask for a phone number. Being able to contact someone at home or on their mobile can be a godsend as it saves your traipsing down to training grounds just to ask one or two minor questions. It can also be a major bonus when an unexpected story breaks and you need to get reaction from the people involved. If you are the freelancer that comes up with the all-important quote you will be the freelancer that cashes in. But understandably sportsmen and women are not keen on dishing out their phone numbers to everyone, so when you ask adhere to the following rules:

- Promise not to give it to anyone else.

- Explain you will not ring every day.

- Give your card in return.

Mullock has a contacts book full of numbers that he has built up over the years, but he still uses a tried and tested method when he needs to ask for yet another number:

'You need to build up a good rapport first, but once that is in place the best time to ask is at the end of an interview. I just ask if I can take a phone number in case there is anything I have missed.'

But if the player is reluctant to give you their number, be gracious and back away politely. Don't start a stand-up row as there will only be one loser and it won't be the sports star. I have found it works to back away, saying, 'Don't worry, I can always catch you after training.' Saying that gives the player a way of walking away without hurting your feelings and you have nipped a potentially embarrassing situation in the bud.

Finding the perfect opportunity to make contact

'Press conferences are the curse of the modern game.'

Bobby Robson

When you first start out it is very much a case of following your target into the bar or waiting outside a changing room and fighting for their attention with the numerous people who want to speak to them, be it friends, other players or committee members. But the further up the ladder you go the more organised things become. Professional football managers have set days for press conferences when a gaggle of journalists are invited to the rundown training ground to chat in a pokey office over a cup of foul-tasting coffee. When new players are announced members of the press are sometimes invited to meet them and indulge in a battle of wills with various other media, like television and radio, for their pound of flesh. On these occasions players are primed to talk and you will find you get much better results at press conferences than just turning up after a match on a wing and a prayer.

GAINING THEIR TRUST

'In Czechoslovakia there is no freedom of the press and in England there is no freedom from the press.'

Martina Navratilova

There is an old saying, 'softly, softly catchee monkey', and so it is in building up a relationship with a professional sportsperson. The more they see your face the more they will open up to you, just as with any sort of friendship. But don't overdo it and spend your time constantly bothering them or they will soon tire of indulging you. The more you interview people the more they will tell you, but ensure you don't use the information in ways that can damage the friendship.

For example, if they tell you something that is controversial check with them whether it is 'on the record', or okay to use. If they say 'no', it doesn't matter how much money you could make from selling the quote, scrub it out of your notebook in thick black pen, because if your friend sees it in print they will be your friend no longer.

Paul's advice

Gaining the trust of a player is hard, as Liverpool and England midfielder Paul Ince reveals:

'You can never trust a journalist as far as I am concerned. Obviously there are some you can give fuller answers to than others, but I don't trust many people. That comes from the fact I know a lot of journalists ask questions just so they can get a headline from me. I might say one line, and it is completely blown out of context to make a headline. That really annoys me and I find myself having to think what I'm going to say before I say it. I got caught out that way a lot of times in my younger days, so I'm all for the young pros attending seminars where they are taught how to deal with the media.

But you still have to talk to the media to get through to our fans. It is hard because I find that the media are always against you. If I've played badly, then I'm man enough to take it, but sometimes they write rubbish for the sake of it, just to keep themselves in a job or make a headline and that really winds me up. They're always trying to put players down instead of backing us.'

ASKING FOR STORIES WITHOUT OFFENDING

'A friend in need is a friend indeed' and unfortunately your relationships with your contacts mean you are the one constantly in need, but by building up solid friendships you can still get the information you desire. Don't forget sport players, especially non-professionals, are very keen to get their name in print themselves and will be more than willing to help out. But follow these guidelines to ensure you never offend when asking about a story:

- Never ask too often.

- Tell them you don't mind if they won't tell you.

- Tell them exactly which publication the story is for.

- Never put your contact on the spot with a question.

It's not a walk in the park
Even if you follow all the advice in this chapter to the letter you will still find it hard to build up a good relationship with everyone you meet. Some stars simply don't like the press and others, for one reason or another, will not like you. Do not get put off as for every star who refuses you an interview there will be another who willingly stops for a chat.

Roy's advice

There are other factors, which former Blackburn, Inter Milan and Swiss national team boss Roy Hodgson explains can make it difficult:

'I think it is still part of the game where players, managers and journalists can build up relationships. But freelancers may have problems because they are working for papers who will only buy their stories if the stories are salacious. Personally I don't do a lot of work with freelance journalists because once or twice in the past, and especially with the Swiss national team, a freelance journalist asked for an interview and asked quite sensible questions and there was no problem with the interview. But when it was printed in the newspaper it had a scandalous headline. The journalist was the first to come to me to apologise and say he didn't do that, but if you are a freelance journalist someone has to buy your stuff and they are not going to buy the stuff I am going to tell you.

So either you have to change what I say or find an emphasis which I haven't put on it. So that is the problem for freelance journalists, unless they can get their work into a serious newspaper who will take it as a bona fide interview. But when many newspapers commission freelance people, all they are really doing is protecting their own journalists by letting them get the quotes without harming the relationship between the manager in question and his regular contact.'

Although he believes it is hard, Hodgson does think it is possible to make an impression on sports stars:

'Freelancers can make a good impact by the quality of their questions, by their preparation, by their manner and by their desire to establish a rapport.'

And he does not feel there are questions that journalists should avoid asking:

'I think being a journalist there are no questions that you shouldn't ask. But I think by the tone of the voice in which you ask them you can make a difference in getting a response. If you can show you are asking a question in a sympathetic way and do not show a total lack of empathy as if to suggest you know all the answers, people will respond.'

CASE STUDIES

Clever Andy impresses the desk

Andy hears through one of his Sunday League team-mates that a star player from the local football club is spending one evening a week coaching a junior team in the area. Keen to show the sports desk he is eager for work, he heads off to the training night and once the session is finished politely asks the player for an interview on his extra-curricular training. The player is happy to talk and Andy also gets some good quotes about Saturday's game that the sports editor on the local paper is happy to use.

Jane strikes back with an exclusive

Determined to make her mark, Jane heads to her local squash club where the county's number one and former England international is drinking at the bar. She is granted an interview and finds out the squash star has decided to quit the game because of an injury. The story is news to the squash title that had earlier snubbed Jane and they agree to take ten paragraphs of copy. She is ecstatic as her perseverance and a lucky break have helped her finally break through, and she even got a phone number into the bargain.

CHECKLIST

1. Who would you classify as a contact?

2. Where is the best place to find future contacts?

3. How do you get a contact to trust you?

4. What is a good point of first contact with a club?

5. When should you ask your contact for their phone number?

7

Preparing for Match Day

ENJOYING THE BIG MATCH ATMOSPHERE

There is nothing to beat the feeling of a match day. Whether it be players, fans or journalists, it is hard to contain the excitement as you wait for the big occasion. This is what you are in the business for – to watch two teams play out a game in a sporting arena that could turn into one of the best memories or pay-days in your life. And I can guarantee that when you first face up to the occasion you will have as many butterflies in your stomach as the stars you are about to watch. There will be so many fears and worries buzzing around your brain it will be hard to think straight. The hairs on your neck will be bolt upright like soldiers on parade and you will struggle to hold your pen still. It is a feeling you will never forget and learn to love.

BACK AT BASE

You are in the privileged position of being asked to enter a sports occasion for free and voice your opinions about the event for potentially thousands of people to read. But it is back in the office where the real work is done. You have your role, which I will explain as the chapter unfolds. But you are possibly one of a hundred journalists working for the paper that day, so to give you an oversight on how you fit into the grand scheme of things, I have outlined below some pointers to show how the day unfolds in the office. A Saturday on a national sports desk is busy so we will use that as our example:

- Pages are designed with each event allocated its own space.

- Reporters ring in to receive their order from the desk.

- Chunks of copy are sent to the desk at specific times – frequently before the end of the match.

- Sub-editors check the copy and place it into the appropriate space.

- Phone calls are made to chase missing or erroneous copy.

- Further calls are put out with desks asking for rewrites or checks on facts.

- The paper is put to bed.

As you can see, the desk of a paper on a match day is chaotic to say the least, which means you can earn brownie points by delivering your copy on time and in good shape.

DRESSING TO IMPRESS

Although all the fun begins on match day, you should begin your work far earlier than the kick-off time and I would suggest you make your preparations for the game the night before to ensure things go smoothly. Begin by thinking about what you are going to wear because if you believe a pair of jeans and T-shirt will suffice you are wrong! You are now a professional person in a professional trade and wearing your leisure clothes will only count against you. Next time you look around a press box see what people are wearing. The men in trousers and ties and women in smart outfits are the professionals, while the guys and girls in jeans are there for their own pleasure. You will notice this and so can the players and managers and you find the reporters dressed smartly are the ones who are treated with more respect and get the story.

KNOWING YOUR FACTS AND FIGURES

Doing a little bit of homework before travelling to the game will add depth to your subsequent report. Minor details can make you sound more authoritative in your reporting and in the hurly-burly before the match you will struggle to find time to get out your record books. A press room before a game is no place to study. White-haired reporters will be milling about offering their advice on the latest sporting scandal through puffs of cheap cigarette smoke to anyone who listens. And you will be more concerned with saving your seat from the arrogant journalists who turn up late and pick on the newest face they spot to bully for a place to perch their oversized bottoms.

So on the night before the game, here are some things to look for:

- top scorers for both sides

- last time either player or team lost

- biggest win or defeat

- highest ranking of both players/teams

- where each side could end up in the table.

Local papers are always handy for this sort of information and the details are normally written in a preview the night before the game. Also check past programmes and the Saturday sports specials that many newspapers print after games for useful titbits.

If you are covering a smaller event there will be a lot less pressure on you pre-match and you can ask around for information when you get there.

WHEN TO ARRIVE

You can never arrive too early for a game, only too late – and that can sound the death knell for your career. I once misjudged my timings and arrived 15 minutes after kick-off for a clash between Sheffield Wednesday and Leeds. My late arrival caused me to miss the opening goal of the game. A fellow hack explained how the goal came about but I was never comfortable with the report I filed and vowed that day I would never be late again. I now aim to get to a game 60 minutes before kick-off as this allows me time to relax and get my mind thinking about the match.

Matt's advice

Matt Lawton is the *Daily Express's* Manchester United correspondent and he has a set routine for match days that has helped him rise to the top in his profession:

'I like to get to a game an hour before the kick-off as it gives me a chance to go through the programme and check if there is anything in it that I need to know. I also like to have a chat with contacts at the ground to make sure I know exactly what has been going on since I was last there. Getting there early gives me a chance to relax a bit as well, as there is nothing worse than turning up for a game when the ref has a whistle in his mouth ready for kick-off. Doing that leaves you open to make mistakes.

Before I set off I make sure I look smart so I can earn the respect of football people I am going to talk to. Most managers wear shirt and tie and if you turn up in jeans and a T-shirt they will not take you as seriously as someone who looks like a professional. Although I am dressed smartly I always make sure I will be warm. There is nothing worse than trying to work when you are freezing.'

STUDYING THE TEAM SHEETS AND PROGRAMMES

Obviously at minor events you are not given team sheets and programmes so it a case of talking to the press officer before the clash.
But where available always read the manager's notes in the programmes as sometimes you find he makes a point that is more important than the game itself. He may be answering a critic or explaining
why he sold the club's prize asset. You won't be the only person to
spot the story, but you may be the only person to miss it if you forget to look.

Nearer kick-off time at bigger games you will have to jostle with
the press pack for one of the limited number of team sheets that are
handed out. The sheet lists the players in action. Check the names
against the biogs in the programme for interesting background information. One of the visitors may have played at the home club for a
few years, and if they score in the game it will give you something to
write about. You can also use the team sheets to help you during
games by marking down formations, bookings and replacements. For
an example, see Figure 2.

WORKING IN THE PRESS BOX

To a sports writer there are few places in the world better than a
busy press box on a Saturday afternoon. As soon as you enter you
will find a workplace like no other. Over the space of the next couple of hours this small-constricted area with tight seating and a small
collection of grubby overused phones will turn into a place of wonder to the unacquainted. From the early afternoon camaraderie to
final whistle chaos the press box is a heaven for a capable journalist
and hell to the poor scribe.

There are four types of press box inhabitant and it is helpful to
know whom to steer clear of for an easier life. Below is a rough guide
for you to follow during your first few games.

1. The Old Gent
In every box there are the old gents who have been there, seen it all
and offer an opinion on every incident. They will want to grab your
phone just when you need it most and have the cheek to ask you to
do their legwork for them. Avoid them like the plague.

2. The Pack
Also in attendance will be the pack of wolves who will exclude you

Football WALES

Euro 2000 Group One Qualifying Match

Wales v Italy
Anfield, Liverpool
Saturday, 5th September 1998, kick off 7.45 p.m.

	Wales			Italy	
1	Jones		1	Peruzzi	
2	Robinson		2	Panucci	
3	Barnard		3	Pessotto	
4	Symons		4	Baggio D	
5	Williams -		5	Connavaro	
6	Coleman – 40th CAP		6	Juiliano	
7	Johnson		7	Fuser GOAL 16min	
8	Speed		8	Albertini	
9	Blake Y Curd 25min		9	Vieri - GOALS BEAT ASTON VILLA IN UEFA CUP	
10	Hughes – CAPTAIN.		10	Del Piero	
11	Giggs		11	Di Franceso	
12	Bellamy -sub for 9 (74min)		12	Buffon	
13	Saunders		13	Negro	
14	Trollope		14	Serena	
15	Mardon		15	Di Biago	
16	Llewellyn		16	Inzaghi	
17	Savage		17	Chiesa	
21	Ward		18	Baggio R sub for 10 (68mins)	

Referee: Hauge — NORWEGIAN

Reserve Official: Olsen

Assistant Referee: Sundet
Borgan

Plymouth Chambers, 3 Westgate Street, Cardiff CF1 1DD. Tel: 01222 372325

Fig. 2. Example of a team sheet.

at every turn. These are the big boys who generally write for nationals or large regional papers. They are paranoid that you will steal their best angle and will want to stop you listening to any player's opinion. Introduce yourself to them and expect to be ignored – only after months of seeing you around will they finally acknowledge your existence.

3. The Smiley People
The third type of press box species write for little known weekly papers and are great company and useful to ask for information. But don't get dragged into their world of doing the minimum to get by – you won't make any money if you fall into that trap.

4. The Press Association
At most higher profile events there is always someone present reporting for the Press Association. As you will have read earlier, they will give the official line to the world, so it is a good idea to find out who they are so you can ask them how they are going to call any important situation. At least then your report will match the only other view seen by the sports editor of the day.

ONCE THE ACTION HAS BEGUN

This is where the hard work and the fun begin. From here on in it is important to keep your eyes peeled and pencils sharp.

How to watch a game
Whenever you play a sport you are always taught to watch the ball, be it cricket, football, squash or whatever. When you learn to report on sports matches there is another rule to learn – 'watch the ball and everyone else on the pitch'. Sounds hard, doesn't it? And let's make no bones about it – it is. But with a lot of practice it is an art you can and will have to master.

The flying winger may be haring in for a try under the posts, but will you spot the second row punching his rival 50 yards back – forcing the referee to disallow the try? Even though you may be crammed into a tiny press box with people either side of you screaming copy into mobile phones, **you still needed to see it**.

There is no simple rule to learning how to spot everything, it's something you pick up as you go along. To begin with, though, ask the person next to you as they may have spotted the incident – that is, if they are not too busy themselves.

WRITING THE MATCH REPORT

Depending on who you are writing for, there are several types and styles you have to adhere to when writing match reports. Here are the three you are most likely to come across:

1. *The runner.* A blow-by-blow account of the game used by papers that run Saturday evening or Sunday editions. The same style of report is used when covering a night match. For an example, see Figure 3.

2. *The measured piece.* A report that is built around quotes from the key players in the game. It is usually filed the following day and concentrates more on the implications of the match than the action. This is generally because sports fans will have seen the talking point of the game on television.

3. *The follow-up.* An article that is asked for from papers the day after an evening event that has been covered by a runner. It looks at the implications of the match and carries no match action.

Writing a runner

Probably the biggest fear of any sports writer is producing a runner for the first time. It is also one of the most satisfying feelings to have completed one. This is a match report that you file to a copy-taker while the game is in progress. The whole process is finished on the final whistle.

To be good at a runner it is simply a case of keeping cool and passing on what you see to a copy-taker. This sounds easy but can be hard when you are trying to make notes and watch a game at the same time. You could be jotting down the details of a goal or try when another score happens. Or there could be a major fight with a dozen players involved. The game won't stop while you catch up. A runner is real rollercoaster stuff and a sure-fire way to sort the good from the bad.

Working your notepad

The most common way to make notes during a game is to buy an A4-size notepad and draw a line down the centre of the page. On the left-hand side write the home team's name and the visiting team on the right. As the match continues write down any important moments for each team on their side of the page. This method allows you at a glance to pick out the incidents needed to write your report. See Figure 4.

Roy rocked by Dazza

LIVERPOOL.........1
COVENTRY.........3

ROY EVANS has slammed his dodgy Liverpool defence for conceding three crazy goals on a day of shame for the Anfield giants.

Liverpool's backline was torn apart by a dynamic Darren Huckerby whose brilliant display could even leave Evans facing the sack.

Boss Evans will now continue his search across Europe to find a quality defender the Reds backline is crying out for.

But any signings will come too late for the crucial Coca-Cola Cup game at Newcastle in midweek where defeat would leave their season in tatters.

Huckerby scored one and set up the other two as his electric pace gave Coventry a cutting edge Liverpool never enjoyed.

And with only Jamie Redknapp's early free kick to cheer, Liverpool left the pitch to a chorus of boos and calls for Evans' head.

Evans said: "We won't have any complaints about it and we have to give Coventry credit for what they've done. They outfought us, were quicker to the ball and we failed to respond.

"We were never in control of the game even at 1-0. They were into us quickly and we were second best.

"The goals were crazy. The defensive position is very worrying for us, especially when you concede goals like we did.

Surprise

"We didn't defend the goals well at all and some of them we handed over on a plate."

Liverpool had made the perfect start with Redknapp impressive in midfield.

It was no surprise when the Reds took a sixth-minute lead.

Karl-Heinz Riedle, back in place of food-poisoned Michael Owen, was barged off the ball by Paul Williams on the edge of the City box.

With Paul Ince lining up a 25-yard blaster, Redknapp cheekily nipped in to curl in an effort that Magnus

By Jeremy Butler

Hedman could only palm into his net.

The equaliser came on the stroke of half-time as Huckerby picked up the ball on the left.

He produced a series of sidesteps to leave Bjorn Kvarme and Dominic Matteo in his wake as he ran at goal.

And with David James charging out he lofted the ball into the far corner.

Then James could only parry his thunderous 62nd-minute shot and Dion Dublin gratefully snatched his 10th of the season.

In the dying moments the electric Huckerby latched onto another loose ball and curled in a deflected shot against the post.

Paul Telfer was the happy recipient this time to ram the ball past James.

Evans and Coventry boss Gordon Strachan agreed referee Mike Riley had gaffed in not awarding the Reds a 33rd-minute penalty.

Coventy midfielder George Boateng took out Steve Harkness at waist height in the box but the Leeds official mystified the home fans by waving away appeals for a spot kick.

Liverpool midfielder Ince groaned: "Losing at home to Coventry is a huge blow but you've got to point a finger at the whole team.

"We let down the fans, the staff and ourselves."

Fig. 3. Example of a runner from the *News of the World*.

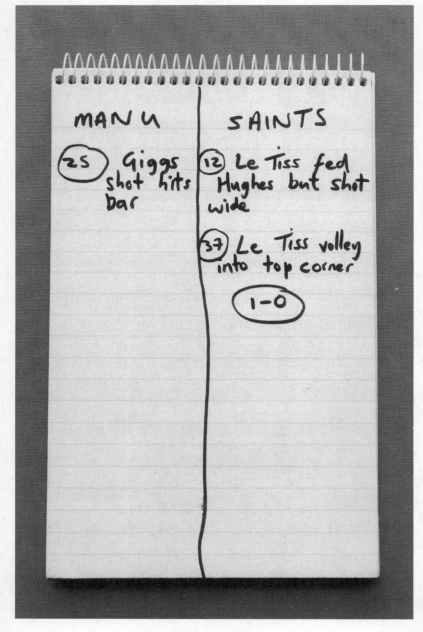

Fig. 4. Working your notepad.

Note elaborating

Write down quick notes on your pad about the action and when the time comes to talk to copy simply elaborate on them. For example, I would write down, '23 Windass shot wide after good ball from Abbott'. And when I am talking to copy I would say, 'Windass wasted a great opportunity to open the scoring in the 23rd minute when he blasted wide after being put through on goal by an accurate Abbott pass.'

Using longhand

An alternative is to write your report in longhand, as you would expect to see it printed in the paper. It is tricky to do this while still watching the game, but if you are not confident about your ability to file your report 'off the cuff', longhand is the best option.

Chris's advice

In his role as a sports editor, Chris Harvey has spent many Saturday afternoons and Monday mornings hoping the freelance copy he has ordered is delivered on time and to his satisfaction:

> 'The key is making sure the copy I receive is clean. On a busy Saturday, for instance, you don't want to be messing about looking up how to spell a player's name. You want the freelance to have checked out the names and facts before the copy is sent to you.
>
> It's also vital that it arrives on time and is the length you have asked for. I don't mind it coming in a little bit too long, but never to short. If the copy is coming for Monday's paper they can afford to be more descriptive with their work and can make it a bit more flowery in style. But as long as they have the right facts in the right order and it arrives at the right time there is really little I will complain about.'

Earning your corn

When you are starting out, your experiences of doing a runner will be restricted to filing four or five paras onto copy on a Saturday afternoon for a regional paper. But as I am convinced there is no reason why a good freelancer should not end up writing for the national newspapers, I will give you an insight into how tricky things can get in the big league. I once covered the Premiership clash between Barnsley and Crystal Palace for three papers – the *News of the World*, the *Daily Express* and the *Sunday Sport*. This was my brief:

- The *NoW* wanted 400 words at half time, 250 at three-quarters-time and a five-para intro five minutes from the end plus marks for individual players in each team.

- Then they wanted four paras each on four different aspects of the match – shot, save, move and man of the match, and a few lines on the referee.

- They also wanted two 600-word rewrites from each side's point of view with manager's quotes included by 6 pm.

- The *Express* wanted 500 words on the whistle and a quotes rewrite of the same length.

- The *Sport* asked for a straight ten-para match report.

Bearing in mind I had to take time away from filing copy to collect the quotes and speak to a few players so I could do a Monday piece for the *Express*, you can see it was quite a day.

Writing measured pieces

This is the other type of match report that you see in the national papers on a Monday or in the local press during the week. If you are starting out you will generally write for local papers and if it is a Saturday match they will want your report on the Sunday at the earliest. For this style of report, jot down in your notepad the major incidents of the game with the time they occurred. When it comes to writing the report – and it is better to write it as soon as possible after the game – follow these six simple rules:

1. *Avoid the weather report.* Never start with a description of the weather. It is the biggest mistake a new freelancer can make and will bring plenty of mocking from the sports desk. You are writing a sports report not a novel.

2. *Key moment.* Start with the key moment of the game – a goal or a sending off or a debatable penalty. If possible try and pinpoint the people involved and write around them. Obviously it is easy if someone has won a tennis match you are reporting on, though it can prove difficult in other sports. But if a player scores the winner he is the person to build your piece around, and if you can speak to him afterwards and pick up some quotes all the better.

3. *Picking out the best bits.* Reserve the first three paras for a sparkling introduction and then mentions of other scorers or most

important parts of the game and leave the quotes till later. How do you know what the important parts are, I hear you cry! Think of the most exciting aspect of the action and that is your introduction. Figure 5 shows two introductions I have written for papers to give you a guide to how it should be done.

4. *Using quotes.* If you have a reaction from players or managers make sure it goes high up in the article and illustrates the point being made. Your piece will sound silly if your intro talks about a possible penalty and the manager's or players' quotes kick off talking about how the result affects the league position. Make sure each quote relates directly to the incident mentioned in the copy. For example:

> Ron Jones was forced to the ground by a rugby style mauling from defender Andy Roberts, but referee Paul Hart ignored the claims for a penalty. Jones later complained: 'I can't believe the ref didn't give it. He was all over me.'

5. *Finishing power.* Once you have the quotes out of the way, the rest of the match report depends on length and the date the paper uses the copy. When you are starting out most papers will only want a few paragraphs so you will have to write tight copy at this point. People hitting the post or shooting just wide must be jettisoned to get in the most important points.

6. *Size is important.* Don't over- or under-write as this will upset the sub-editors. Too much means time is wasted rewriting the copy and too little leaves a hole that has been filled. Stick as close as you can to the length ordered. A few words over is okay, but don't ever drop under the amount requested.

> **Never forget**: All the paper you are working for wants is the facts in copy that doesn't have to be rewritten. If you supply them with it they will use you again – and that is the name of the game.

National papers

If you are writing for the Monday edition of a national paper, a similar style to the one we've discussed above would be pointless as most people would have either seen the goals or read about the game in a Sunday paper. In this case you need to pick out the most explosive point of the game and open with that. From there the majority of the piece is built around the quotes from the key players in the game. Keep the actual action to a few paragraphs at the end that includes

Dario hits unlucky 13

DARIO GRADI admits he has run out of ideas about how to stop Crewe's speedy slide back into the Second Division.

Goals in each half from Gavin Peacock and Mike Sheron meant Alex have now gone 13 games without a victory.

It would have been a lot worse but for some sloppy finishing from the resurgent Londoners. A desperate Gradi said: "I've got problems and we must win soon.

"But it would be stupid to make predictions as to how we will get out of our present trouble, because at the moment I just don't know.

"We deserved to lose and on chances created they should have been 3-0 up at half-time."

Crewe started brightly, with skipper Shaun Smith drilling a free-kick just wide with Ludek Miklosko well beaten.

But then a rickety offside

CREWE · 0
QPR · 2

By Jeremy Butler

trap broke down. David Walton cleared off the line from Kevin Gallen and Jason Kearton bravely denied Sheron. But the escapes could not go on and Peacock waltzed through another bungled offside ploy for a clinical finish in the 33rd minute.

Steve Anthrobus came on to cause QPR some problems with his bustling style but wasted Crewe's best chance to get back into the game, prodding the ball wide from eight yards after Rodney Jack had set up the chance.

The miss proved costly, with Sheron's stunning overhead kick sailing past the stranded Kearton to seal the points for QPR in the 62nd minute.

Crewe slip into gear as Westwood shines

OXFORD came to the home of Rolls Royce with two old Fords and a Banger – and paid for their lack of quality.

A brilliantly-created Ashley Westwood goal and a Steve Anthrobus header earned Dario Gradi's side their first win in eight games.

Crewe had to come from behind after Mike Ford headed home a 14th-minute free-kick from namesake Rob, following a foul on Nicky

CREWE 2
OXFORD 1

Banger. But they drew level when defender Westwood carried the ball 60 yards before finding Colin Little, then raced on to tap home the winger's cross.

Little also created the 41st-minute winner, providing a perfect cross for Anthrobus to nod home.

Fig. 5. Examples of intros from the *News of the World* and *Sunday Express*.

the scorers and the times of the scores. Read a few nationals on Monday for examples.

Writing a follow-up

You will only have to worry about follow-ups when you are working for national papers and covering a mid-week game. The theory is simple; after deciding on the flash point of the game, find someone to talk about it other than the managers.

A manager will already have spoken to the Press Association and his quotes will be out long before your article hits the streets. In practice, while you are filing copy, attending managers' press conferences and adding their words to your piece, the players are usually jumping into their cars and heading for home. It is a case of Jack be nimble, and Jack have a few friends in the press pack willing to help you. For an example, see Figure 6.

Matt's advice

There are a few key factors you need to follow if you intend to keep the sports desk happy on a match day. Matt explains:

'When you are writing a runner, all the desk care about in the first instance is getting their copy in time. But it isn't enough just to make sure you are prompt, because once they've got it they will then start moaning about the quality if the writing isn't up to scratch. The trick is to supply good copy and get it to the desk on time. Then there can be no complaints.

I like to write as I go along and think up an idea for an intro

Hendrie blows his top

By JEREMY BUTLER
Crewe 3 Barnsley 1

SEAN McClare grabbed a debut goal for Barnsley but would have swapped his big moment for a result which might have saved a post-match dressing down.

Barnsley player-boss John Hendrie laid into his men after defeat in a game they should have won.

McClare said: "I can't tell you what the manager said but he wasn't a happy chappy."

Shaun Smith gave Crewe a dream start from the penalty spot before McClare, on as a 41st minute substitute for the injured Georgi Hristov, fired home shortly after the interval.

Then Crewe's own supersub, Chris Lightfoot, capitalised on two bouts of bad defending to give Alex their first win of the season.

Barnsley striker Ashley Ward said: "We've got a lot of work to do and we'll start doing that work now.

"Today was just a poor performance. We are determined to get back up. We've sampled the Premier League and want to go back there.

"It's early days yet. We've won one, drawn one, and lost one so we haven't had a terrible start."

Fig. 6. An example of a follow-up.

towards the end of the game. If there has been a major incident it makes life easier because you can lead off on that. But if there isn't you need to put more thought into it. Pick out an aspect you think is particularly relevant and craft your intro so it introduces the readers into a train of thought you are working towards.

It is different when you are writing a follow-up piece for a Monday paper. I watch out for the major talking point in the game and afterwards try and find the players, managers and officials who were involved and get their opinion. I like to use the most powerful opinion to get the ball rolling in my report and then blend the other views into it.'

HOW TO FILE COPY

To start with you can begin filing copy by the greatest invention known to the sportswriter – the telephone. Slightly slow and laborious it may be, but when all other mechanical inventions go wrong the phone is always there to bail you out.

Once you are more established you can move onto the laptops and file using the Newslink service discussed earlier. When you sign up to Newslink they will provide all the details you need to make sure your copy arrives safely. When you are starting out a laptop is frankly an unnecessary expense.

Here are the golden rules to filing copy by phone:

- Check the paper will have copy-takers on at the times you want to file.

- Ensure you take the phone number for copy with you to games.

- Tell the typist which publication the report is for.

- Make sure you spell out all complicated names.

- Don't forget to give the score.

- Fifteen minutes after your call contact the sports desk to make sure the copy has reached them.

CASE STUDIES

Andy's league debut

Andy has been given the nod to cover his first professional league game for his local paper after months of pleading. He has been asked to provide ten paragraphs of the Hull versus Scarborough game plus a follow-up. During the game a controversial goal is given and the old gent at the back of the press box claims the Rochdale number nine thumped the Hull goalkeeper. Andy has not seen the incident but is worried about missing something important and includes it in his copy. It is something he should not have done. He neither knows nor can trust the old gent. He should have mentioned a collision between the pair and checked with one of the players later. It is the perfect tale for a follow-up.

Jane scores at her local squash club

On the back of her story in the squash magazine Jane has managed to persuade a national paper to take three paragraphs of copy on the local squash championships on her patch. But when she gets there she realises she does not have enough background knowledge. On arrival she immediately finds the club's press officer, who is so excited by the fact a national paper is interested in their outfit, he sits beside her throughout the match. Her report is perfect and she is asked to cover a similar event the following week.

CHECKLIST

1. What should you wear to matches?

2. At what time should you arrive for the game?

3. Why should you read the programme?

4. If you need information, who is the best person to contact?

5. What is the difference between a measured piece and a runner?

6. What makes a good intro?

7. What information should you never leave out of a report?

8. In which ways can you file copy?

8

Writing General Sports Stories

SAVING YOURSELF FROM STARVING

It's hard to beat being at a game for all the spills and drama of late goals, tension-packed come-from-behind wins and tear-filled winning returns from career-threatening injuries. But if you plan to take this business seriously and do not want to starve you to have to find something to do during the week. In fact when you are working at the top end of the market most national papers will not consider you for match reporting until you can prove you can write by supplying them with sports stories. So in this chapter we will look at how to track down stories and how to make them attractive to newspaper desks.

FINDING THE STORIES

A few years ago I met a fat Scotsman with a large beard and belly to match. He ran his own news agency and he let me in on an important secret. When he was about to take on a new member of staff he always arranged to meet them in their local pub. He got there first and when the candidate walked in he watched closely and if the barman or one of the other drinkers didn't acknowledge him as a friend he knew instantly he couldn't employ him.

'You won't get stories sat at home watching telly. You need to be in a pub to find out what is going on,' he growled.

Now I'm not suggesting you turn into an alcoholic but the point is it's hard finding stories unless you are out and about. Popping into the bar at your local football and rugby club every now and then helps. At every club there is the local gossip or a disgruntled player who is willing to let you know what is happening behind the scenes. Even if you can't find them, once they know you write for the local paper it won't be long before they approach you.

And obviously it is worth keeping in contact with the sports stars you have befriended because they will be in the know and, if you treat them right, will give you a hand every now and then.

HOW TO WRITE STORIES

Ensuring accuracy

'and there is the unmistakable figure of Joe Mercer . . . or is it Lester Piggot?'

Brough Scott

Before we go any further in this chapter it is vital you grasp the most important concept of journalism – accuracy. Forget such ill-founded claims as 'don't let the facts ruin a good story'. If you ignore the facts it could be the ruin of your budding career. From checking the spelling of names to ensuring the subject matter of the story is correct, getting things right is a must before you send a story to any publication.

Grabbing interest

A sports news editor does not spend his day with his feet up on his desk waiting for your story to pop onto his screen so he can dissect it and make sure he has not missed an important point. Never forget your tale will get a quick once over like an experienced car dealer inspecting a second-hand motor he is thinking of buying, and if it does not come up to scratch it will be sent into the spike queue and never seen again. So it is important to remember the three key items a story needs to catch a sports news editor's eye:

- It contains a fact he does not know.

- It is about a big name in the sport you are writing about.

- It is a controversial tale.

If you can produce a story with any of these three factors you have a fair chance of seeing your tale in print. If all three are covered, give yourself a big pat on the back. While the first two points are good sellers the controversial story is always an excellent one to pick up on. No decent sports news editor will ignore a tale about two different groups of people arguing – just look at the amount of column inches Dutch football player Pierre Van Hooijdonk filled when he refused to come back to Nottingham Forest and went on strike. On a lesser scale your local paper will welcome a tale about a club moaning because they have been kicked out of a competition for a reason they believe is wrong.

Finding an angle

Unfortunately not every story you produce will be blessed with one of the three points we have just mentioned. So it is important to ensure every piece you send to a paper has a decent angle to it. An angle or 'line' is journalism speak for 'what the story is about'. To find the best angle, grab a clean sheet of paper and write down every interesting fact you have picked up about the story in bullet points. Pick out the most eye-catching fact as that will be your intro and then number the rest of the facts in descending order of importance. But make sure you've got the best line because if you've picked the wrong angle you could well find no one is interested in your story. In Figure 7 the angle was easy to pick up as Lars Bohinen had seen his transfer request accepted.

How do you find the best angle?

Of course, you are now dying to know what makes something the most eye-catching fact in your tale. Unfortunately the only way to find out is through experience and having a nose for a tale, but there is always a simple test which will help you during the beginning of your career. Imagine you are telling a story to a friend in the pub about the best football match you have ever seen. You wouldn't start by telling him the name of the referee would you? You would go straight into explaining the most dramatic moment like a last-minute winning goal. Think of your stories in the same way. Think, 'If I was telling my friend in the pub about this story, how would I start?' Your answer to that question is your intro.

Writing the intro

Sports stories are a totally different art to writing match reports and it takes quite a bit of skill and, of course, that old bug bear – practice – to get it right. When you are penning a report you can pretty much guarantee its target audience will read it whether or not you have produced a killer intro. You will be writing about the reader's team and they will be desperate to know why their side were soundly beaten or how they captured a scalp in a shock cup result. With a general story the reader's interest level will not be so high and you need to catch them with a killer intro that will force them to spill their coffee in their lap as they grab hold of their paper.

A good intro can sell a poor story and a poor intro can kill a good story. Getting it right is a trick that is easier said than done, so remember the following points:

• Be short, sharp and to the point.

• Don't try and be too clever.

• Avoid puns in case your sense of humour is not shared by others.

Lars chance to get away

By JEREMY BUTLER

LARS Bohinen's Blackburn misery is set to end after the club accepted his second transfer request of the season. The Norwegian is worried that lack of first-team action could ruin his chances of making the World Cup finals.

He made his first request six weeks ago and was told to stay and fight for his place. But after further talks with manager Roy Hodgson, the 28-year-old has finally got his wish.

Hodgson admits that he is now willing to sell, but if only if the price is right for a player he rates highly. He said: "Of his type he is the best player in the country at the moment.

"His best position is in behind the front two strikers, but I haven't been able to play him there. We play with two wingers and that means I need two ball-winners in the midfield.

"But we won't be letting him go on the cheap. I would rather keep him, but he wants to play football so he can go to the World Cup and you have to respect his feelings."

Bohinen is out of today's trip to Southampton and Hodgson has worries over virus victims Chris Sutton and Tore Pedersen.

Hodgson, who dismissed reports that he is set to make a bid for Saints' Norwegian international Egil Ostenstad, added: "Sutton has been confined to his bed this week, but Pedersen is not so bad." Defender Stephane Henchoz is also doubtful after damaging a thigh in a midweek reserve match.

Matthew Le Tissier must wait to see if he has done enough to persuade manager David Jones to end his Southampton exile.

He has been dropped for the last two matches, but starred after coming on as a substitute in the midweek defeat against Coventry.

The 29-year-old, currently out of Glenn Hoddle's England plans, has lost half-a-stone after going on a self-imposed regime of extra training.

He looked back to his best against Coventry and Jones must now consider recalling him to face Blackburn.

"If Tiss is honest with himself, he hasn't been at his best for the last 18 months," said Jones, who became the first Southampton manager to drop Le Tissier for four years earlier this season.

"He's really the only one who can snap himself out of the slump he's been in but the signs are there that he's getting back to being the player he was. He has been working hard and he isn't overweight now.

"He's been working really hard on certain elements of his game with some extra training. He could work harder, but he's still an international player with lots of ability.

"Even at his age he can work to improve and he is now doing that."

The absence of leading scorer Kevin Davies could force Jones' hand, with the England under-21 international still struggling to recover from an ankle injury.

Fig. 7. Finding an angle in a piece from *The Express*.

- Don't debate the plus and minus points, just give the facts.
- Ensure your copy is clear, precise and, most importantly, accurate.

The pyramid effect

When you are writing a story, it will inevitably be too long and a kind sub-editor (I am being sarcastic here) will lovingly rewrite it to fit the hole in the paper it is meant to fill.

In reality the sub who picks up your story will have one hundred and one better things to do than check your story is perfect and this means you have to help them as much as you can. They have a hole to fill and in some cases will just chop off anything that doesn't fit. So if you've left an important point until last it will get the chop. To avoid this, think of your writing as a reversed pyramid (see Figure 8) with the most important line at the top and least important at the bottom. Doing this will ensure your best work does see the light of day rather than the computer's recycle bin.

Developing your story

Once you've got your points marked down, put flesh on the bones by using short sentences that contain no waffle. Including in the copy the player's former teams or recent tournaments they have won is

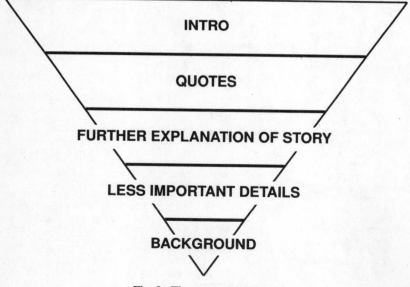

Fig. 8. The pyramid effect.

acceptable – listing the names of the star's children will be laughed at.

Once you have found out the crux of the tale, don't just stop there – think who else might be involved and what the greater implications may be and then approach relevant people for quotes. For example, if a player claims he wants to leave the club, speak to the manager and the chairman to see if they will let him go. If you get a conflict you can even make a double hit out of the story as on one day you can sell a tale about a star wanting to leave the club and the next you can sell another story about the manager telling him he is going nowhere.

It does not have to be on such a grand scale either. If the local squash league decide that a revolutionary new flooring for courts has to be in place for next season, you may find, by ringing round a few clubs, they are up in arms over the cost because it could put them out of business. If you contact the oldest club in the area and they are in the same boat you have a nice little tale brewing.

The life-saving check

When I was taught to drive I was told to glance over my right shoulder before pulling out to overtake a car in front. My driving instructor called it the life-saving check. Now it may sound melodramatic but I like to use my own version of the life-saver on my copy before I wave it goodbye. There are two parts to the process with the first check ensuring that I am accurate, starting with a check on the facts and a spell check. The second part makes sure I have not missed out any vital points. I look through the story to ensure I have told the reader the following:

- **Who** – have I given enough information about the key person in the story?

- **Where** – is the location of the event mentioned?

- **What** – are the details of what went on clearly marked out?

- **When** – have I said when the incident took place?

- **Why** – do I give reasons for what has happened?

Once I have checked that all the above questions have been answered, I feel confident my story is ready to be seen by the cynical eyes of a sports news editor. Sometimes because of the nature of the story you will not be able to answer yes to all the above points, but if you have checked whether there is an explanation for each point you can send the tale without worrying that you have left something vital out. The five-point check can also be used to figure out questions for an interview.

What to leave out

Just because you have spent the last hour finding out all the minor details of a celebrity you do not have to include them all in your story. Only the relevant facts are needed and telling the reader what colour stocks your subject prefers to wear in a story about his desire to win a trophy is taking it too far. By all means use little oddities to add colour to your piece but make sure you are not stuffing your article with incongruous information.

STRENGTHENING YOUR WRITING STYLE

Once all the facts are in place, re-read your story and look for ways of tightening up your copy. You can never go back over your writing enough times as every new inspection will throw up ideas about how you can improve your piece. But do not spend your whole day rewriting and rewriting, as you will never send the story and therefore have no chance of getting paid for it. Although you will learn to hate deadlines and the speed with which they creep up on you, they do have their uses in ensuring you let go of your copy instead of poring over it until it drives you mad with frustration.

One final check that is worth carrying out before sending your copy is reading it out loud. You will be surprised how different certain sentences can sound when they are taken in by your ears rather than your eyes. But quite often you find a sentence, which looked alright on the page, does not sound so good and you will need to correct it.

Consider the points below when you are rewriting your latest story:

- Are the paragraphs too long and stilted? This can be okay if you are writing for a broadsheet but never use a sentence longer than 15 words for a tabloid.

- Have you used the word 'that'? Try and omit it if you can as 'that' tends to be a redundant word. If the sentence needs it try using 'which' instead.

- Try rewriting any awkward-looking sentences by putting the second half first and following it with the first half.

- Do any words look wrong as you scan your work? Grab a Thesaurus and find a new one.

- Have you checked your copy for spelling mistakes?

- Look at sentences that struggle to gel. Is there a noun or a verb in a passive voice trying to carry the sentence? Try rearranging it with an active verb.

- Are you overusing the word 'will'? Instead of saying 'the event will take place' why not try just 'the event takes place'.

- Read your published work to see what changes are made. Note them down as this is the closest you will get to advice.

Avoiding dog words

Have you ever listened to someone's speech and noticed how often they use obviously redundant words like 'basically', 'you know' and 'really'? These are what are known as 'dog words' and they can cause a major annoyance to anyone listening to the speaker. The problem with dog words is that the speaker obviously tends to become deaf when they slip through his lips and has no idea how annoying they can be. Obviously writers also have dog words and you will spot them as you start to write more and more often. Once you have picked up potential dog words in your articles, obviously write them down and pin them above your computer so you use them as little as possible. Obviously this will ensure your readers enjoy your writing rather than give up under the weight of the dog words. By the way, you may have noticed I picked up a dog word in this section. Annoying isn't it?

Kicking out the jargon

Every industry has a host of words which mean nothing to the uninitiated. Journalism and sport are no different. While obvious terms like 'goal' and 'penalty' are well known, there are plenty of other expressions which will leave the layman scratching his head and ultimately giving up reading your piece if you fill your work with unexplained terms. So if you can't be sure your readers will understand a technical term – don't use it.

WRITING QUOTES

Quotes are the most important part of any story you write. They back up what your intro claims and give the whole tale credence and therefore it is important to place them quite high up in your story and never lower than the fourth paragraph. Make sure you blend them into the piece by ensuring they follow on from the last point you made. For example, if you are claiming a player wants to quit a club you could write:

> John Smith has admitted he wants to leave Oxtown United after being left in the reserves for the past three games.
> He said: 'The manager obviously thinks I'm not good enough and reserve team football is not good enough for me.'

Also note the style on quotes. Whichever publication you are writing for, use one of the following forms:

- He said: 'This is a good book.'

- 'What a cracking book,' he said.

- 'I found this book a great read,' revealed Andrew 'and now I intend to write a sports story.'

GIVING A STORY SPIN

'Spin' is a wonderful newspaper term that you will learn to love if you can master it. But be careful, too much spin on a tale and it will fly out of control and cause you considerable problems.

To start with you will be writing straight pieces where you report facts as they are told to you, but the art of spin will in the long run help turn tales, that are dull if written straight, into little money-earning gems. All you need is a good ear, an imaginative brain and the knack of not going too far and ruining a good relationship with a contact. For while giving a tale a little bit of spin could aid its selling potential, giving it too much could turn it into an uncontrollable monster and lead to your best contact ignoring you for ever. And that would be a disaster, as in this business you live and die by your contacts. It is very shortsighted to think that for the sake of the extra few bob a tale like this will bring, you should risk breaking a friendship that could be ever more helpful as your career progresses.

As an example of spin I will tell you about a tale I did about Crewe Alexandra manager Dario Gradi. During an interview he jokingly mentioned he could not sell one of his young starlets because the player's mum would be on the phone complaining. It was music to my ears. Within hours I had told a story about a soccer manager scared to death of selling his star player in case he got attacked by the youngster's mum. The papers loved it!

AVOIDING THE CLICHÉS

Whilst learning to spin a tale allows you to increase your earning potential, filling your copy with clichés will not. Tempting as it is to litter your work with sayings like 'break the deadlock', the quality control department inside your head should put a stop to it immediately. Sports desks viewing your copy will mark you down as someone who can't write and has had to resort to the age-old scribblings that have bogged down their pages for years in order to finish a piece. So instead of taking the easy option why not go the extra mile for your money and use your imagination and come up with a new idea. Not only will it ensure your copy is fresh, it will lead to you developing your own style.

Ten clichés to avoid

- At the end of the day.

- A game of two halves.

- Sick as a parrot.

- Leapt like a salmon.

- Got out of jail.

- Spared his blushes.

- Safe pair of hands.

- Praying for a goal.

- From hero to villain.

- Missed a sitter.

NEVER LOOK BACK

There is a huge market for the future and a tiny one for the past so shun stories that look dated. Write every story as though it is about to happen. You will notice this even in match reports, which by their very nature are all about events in the past. National newspaper reporters have found a way to update them by using a simple device in the introduction. They simply say: 'Smith scored a late winner to ensure City fans were *today* celebrating their first win of the season.'

You can do this with any story including transfer rumours where you can write: 'Southampton expect to make a multi-million bid for Newcastle's star striker later today.' And it can even work with stories at your local cricket club. For example: 'Cricketers at North Ferriby will be forced to wear helmets next season after a vote at the club's AGM last night.'

LAYING OUT A STORY

There is no hard and fast way to lay out your text. Make sure it is readable and typed if possible. Always include a contact phone number and a catchline. If the story runs to more than one sheet, ensure the first sheet has 'more follows' at the bottom of the page and the following page starts with the catchline and the page number after it. Figure 9 is the first sheet of a story and if it spread to a further sheet the next page would start Dublin 2.

USING YOUR BACKGROUND KNOWLEDGE

As you will quickly learn, people don't buy your wonderful prose or clever word plays – if they did I would be broke. What they buy is knowledge, so start arming yourself to the eyeballs with information that can't fail to help you. Once you have found the angle which grabs the interest of the sports news editor, you should ensure you bring your knowledge of the topic to the fore. It will give your story an authoritative feel and therefore more chance of succeeding.

Try and keep a note of:

- a player's previous records
- decisions taken by AGMs
- preceding statements made by stars or administrators
- results and future fixtures.

All of these will give your story more colour and depth and prove to the reader that you are someone who knows your stuff – boosting your credibility at the same time. But where do you get this info? The list below will help:

- build up a reference library at home
- keep a cuttings file
- log onto the internet
- find a local expert in the field to consult.

FAO: Sports Desk

By Jeremy Butler
Contact number . . (0161 000 1212)

Dublin . . .

Roy Hodgson fears Dion Dublin's massive pay demands could scupper his year long mission to bring the Coventry striker to Ewood Park.

The Blackburn boss's 12-month battle to sign the £20,000 a week England international took a step closer to ending in victory yesterday (TUE) when the two clubs agreed a £6.75 million fee.

But a concerned Hodgson admitted he may yet fail to convince Dublin to sign for Rovers because he won't break the club's wage structure to land the player.

Hodgson said: 'We have a wage structure that we try and keep to, it is a very dangerous one in my opinion, but it's still a wage structure.

'I am only hoping the type of wage demands he is going to make are going to be within our bounds.

'I'm not going to be prepared to recommend to Jack Walker that we throw all of our principles and policies out of the window for the player. However much I like him and however much I want him.

'If we can sign him for £6 million on top of Blackburn wages then that is a good deal for us.

'But if it is anything beyond that then I'm afraid we will just have to leave it to the clubs that pay wages that are way out of what we consider to be normal and reasonable.

'We will pay Dion as the top man he is, but unfortunately if he wants more than the Suttons and the Sherwoods of this world then it will be difficult.'

ENDS

Fig. 9. Laying out a story.

WRITING FEATURES

When you sit down to pen a feature you need to put yourself in a totally different frame of mind from the way you think about writing stories. While all the principles we have talked about in this chapter apply, the approach you take to the piece should be different. I like to think of newspaper writing in terms of getting into your car and driving to your destination as quickly as you can, passing all the necessary checkpoints on the way. A feature piece is more of a Sunday drive – you take in all the same checkpoints and reach the same destination but on the way you stop off and enjoy the sights as and when you spot them. For an example of a feature and the softer style of writing involved see Figure 10.

Making your feature sparkle

Writing a feature means the length of words you have to play with is greatly increased so scribbling down a list of facts will soon become dull for the reader. You need to pick out certain points and play with them. Illustrate them with quotes, anecdotes and word pictures. Bring a little colour to your work by talking about the surroundings where the interview took place, or any little idiosyncrasies your subject may have. If they are wearing one red and one blue sock talk about it. You want your reader to feel as though they were sitting beside you while you did the interview and not that the subject was a cardboard cut-out spouting soundbites they have heard before somewhere else.

Try to:

- paint pictures in your readers' minds

- include plenty of background on your subject

- write a softer intro to relax the reader

- describe the surroundings

- find issues that will be new to the reader

- elaborate on older topics to get the full and sometimes untold story.

CASE STUDIES

A touch of spin helps Andy cash in

While at a local football club dinner, Andy hears of a Brazilian youngster keen to come to England on trial. Although he knows the impov-

The picturesque surroundings of Blackburn's Brockhall Village training ground make the perfect backdrop as Tim Flowers poses for the *Total Football* camera in a frozen goalmouth. This is Flowers' domain and while the imposing England keeper rarely struggles to keep out Premiership strikers, today he is having difficulty with the sun.

As the photographer sets up his next shot, Flowers gazes around the chilly countryside to give his eyes a break from the searing light. "Lovely place this," he remarks. "I doubt if there's a better training ground in the country." It's a good job that Flowers enjoys his place of work because, along with his Blackburn teammates, he has been spending more time at Brockhall than normal this season. The arrival of Roy Hodgson last summer caused a major shake-up in the way the former Premiership title holders go about their business. Training sessions were held morning and afternoon before the evenings started to draw in, and an Italian fitness instructor has been hired to get the Blackburn stars into shape.

But you'll hear no complaints from the players, who are thriving again after slipping, momentarily, into the drop zone last season. Flowers reveals that as soon as Hodgson arrived, he knew afternoons in front of the television, or however footballers spend their spare time, were a thing of the past.

"We went on a pre-season trip to Sweden for a fortnight so he could find out about us and vice-versa," he says. "It was intense out there. We had a fortnight with six games thrown in and we trained morning and afternoon every day. It was hard work, but we soon began to realise what he was about and we all realised that we were going to work hard this year.

"He obviously knows exactly the system he likes to play and exactly the way he likes his teams to set out. That's why we train so hard and for so long, because he likes it to be second nature to us. You know what your job is when certain scenarios crop up in the game." The hard work has paid off. Rovers are challenging for the title again and the disorganisation of last term has disappeared. Where there was confusion and doubt, this term there is a structure to Blackburn's play and an attitude that, on the surface, appears more professional.

Hodgson has achieved all of this without splashing vast sums of chairman Jack Walker's cash. In fact, as Flowers is quick to point out, the recent investment in the team has not received for outgoing stars. "Everyone still thinks of Blackburn as Jack Walker and they call us 'Moneybags Rovers'," the 6ft 3in keeper says. "But that is far from the truth, because we've been relatively quiet in the market for the last three years. We've been more of a selling club lately."

Logic suggests that the fact Walker has recouped his outlay on players – and made a tidy profit into the bargain – should mean a few seasons of despair for the Ewood faithful, yet instead the fans are again talking of a title challenge. But even though Blackburn are clinging on to Man Utd's coat-tails, you'll be hard pressed to find a player ready to discuss winning the Championship. The line from the dressing room is simple: a top-six finish and the chance to play in Europe are the targets.

Flowers, for one, is keen to qualify for a European spot so Rovers can make up for the embarrassment suffered during their last Champions' League venture; an inauspicious affair from first to last. "We got some stick last time and maybe we were a little bit green," Flowers admits. "But it's very difficult when you attack a Champions' League campaign and you've got apprentices on the bench.

"We just weren't equipped. We won the league and didn't sign any players. We knew we were going to be in the Champions' League, but the club just knocked off in my opinion. We just went dormant for the summer and it cost us that year. We just weren't good enough to play in the Champions' League. When Liverpool won the title, for example, the first thing they did was buy three big-name players. That was their mentality. That was what we failed to do – and it cost us."

"We'd lost touch with the way game was being played and w were too arrogant to notice it.

Flowers doesn't expect Blackburn to be so naïve again, and despite only having a squad of 18 players, he believes that if the club can't buy in top stars, they have enough youngsters waiting in the wings to ensure a better showing. "Damien Duff has shown us we have a good youth system now and there are a few queueing behind Damien waiting for their chance as well. The reserve side is top of the League and it's a young team; it's not often you get first-team squad players in there."

Fig. 10. A feature on Tim Flowers from *Total Football*.

erished club could not afford his wages he gets the manager to go on record claiming how much they would love him to come to England. Andy knocks up a piece about the club inviting the glamorous player to join them and a national paper loves the oddball slant and uses his story.

Jane's reputation starts to grow

Armed with several cuttings, Jane writes to the titles that had originally snubbed her and finds they are a little more interested in her work now. Her suggestion of writing a sad tale about a woman golfer in her area who lost her husband while playing a round and now claims his death has inspired her to become the county number one is picked up by a sports magazine. She uses the scenery of the golf course to add some colour and depth to the piece and is congratulated by the editor on her feature and promised more work.

CHECKLIST

1. Where can you find sports stories?

2. What is the most important aspect about a story?

3. Which points will grab a sports editor's interest?

4. Write out a piece and check it against the guidelines under 'Strengthening your writing style'. Did you make many changes?

5. Were there many clichés in it?

6. Do you know what your dog words are?

7. Write a feature on a member of your family using background information to make it sparkle.

9

Improving Your Interview Technique

Now you've got an address book full of contacts, you need to know the best way to pick their brains so you have stories to sell. They may well have all the knowledge necessary for you to write a stunning piece but without asking the right questions or pressing the right buttons they won't tell you. For a start they probably don't even know what it is you're after. So before going out into the field it is worth making sure your interview technique is up to scratch.

DRESSING FOR THE OCCASION

We have already touched on what to wear to matches, but clothes are a factor often missed by the interviewer but picked up on with a vengeance by the interviewee. If you turn out with a tatty jumper covered in food stains the interview will not last too long. The same goes if your breath smells like your dog's – have you ever felt like holding a long incisive chat with someone who has breath that could melt metal? You don't need to be in a suit and a tie all the time, but wearing a pair of trousers and a shirt, even just a casual sports shirt, is a must if you want to fit in and gain more credence with your interview target.

USING GOOD BODY LANGUAGE

There are a few tips that can help you put an interviewee at ease during your time with them. Firstly be pleasant, smile and don't be aggressive. In addition:

- Use their name occasionally.

- Don't cross your arms and legs as this acts as a barrier.

- Don't sit too close and invade their personal space.

- Look at them and don't spend your time gazing around the room.

- Keep your dictaphone at a reasonable distance rather than smacking them in the mouth with it.

FIGHTING FOR YOUR RIGHTS

Can you stand up for yourself? If you want to make sure you never miss out on an interview, you are going to have to learn how to. Whilst interviewing the professional at your local golf club will be a civilised affair, the further you go up the food chain in sports writing the harder you will have to work to get your tu'ppeny's worth. Post-match interviews at Premiership football matches these days are more akin to rugby scrums with reporters forming barriers around the stars and using their elbows to keep you away from the action. Some will even spend the whole interview telling you to go away, and making sure in the process you do not hear a money-spinning word drip from the star's mouth. They can do this safe in the knowledge that one of the other hacks will give them the quotes later.

Instilling fear into your rivals

Reporters do not block you from interviews because they do not like you. They are scared you will use the quotes in a publication which hits the streets before theirs does. It is understandable if somewhat annoying, but at least you can take satisfaction from knowing they are scared of little insignificant you. The fear factor will give you a bit of enjoyment for a while but in the end you need to overcome it.

Getting your fair share

There are two ways available to give you a chance of getting your questions answered but neither will guarantee you the perfect interview. The first is to explain to the reporters that your piece is for a lesser title than theirs. They may then let you join their inner circle, although it could take a few attempts for this to succeed. Alternatively wait until they have finished before approaching your target. The major problem with this second method is that the sports star may be fed up with talking and give you the cold shoulder.

GETTING THE INTERVIEW

There are two ways to set up an interview. You can either go through the proper channels and arrange something for a set date, which is a more convenient method though harder to achieve, or you can cold call. Cold calling means waiting around outside a changing room or a sports ground hoping the player you want strolls out soon and is willing to chat. I call it 'cold calling' because by the time the player comes out you will be cold and if, as happens so often at the top level, they do not want to speak, you will be calling them a few names. If you are lucky enough to have a pre-booked interview use the preparation methods I will explain later in the chapter and look forward to an enjoyable time.

Grabbing a star on the hoof

If you are cold calling the best way to get an interview is to approach your subject and ask, 'can I have a quick word?' and wait for a response. If asked, explain who you are writing for and don't open with an obvious question that has been asked one hundred times before as you will immediately 'turn off' your interviewee. Try finding a question they have not been asked before and get them thinking. You will get more respect for coming up with something original and probably get a better than usual answer.

Martin's advice

British Lion captain Martin Johnson believes rugby union players are willing to talk to journalists if they are contacted at the right time:

'I've never known a player not speak to a journalist as it is part and parcel of the game. Obviously if they phone me up on a Sunday night after a match and I'm tired I wouldn't be too happy. But these days most clubs have press officers and if you contact them or in my case my management company I think you find players accommodating. There is always the option of going to a game and speaking to a player after the match. In general, though, I think although the media is interested in rugby there is maybe not so much media pressure in the game and therefore players are quite happy to talk to journalists.'

Arranging a set piece interview

If you are looking for a piece for the local paper the best way to sort out an interview with a sporting star playing regularly in the area is to approach them and ask if you can set a time and date for a chat. But for the bigger names in sport the first place to head is their club. A press officer or the club secretary may be able to help you by getting a message through or informing you of the best time to approach your subject. They may pass you on to the star's agent, but don't be put off by this. The agent's job is to make the player money and the fact you are willing to put them in the spotlight might entice the agent into allowing you some time with his client. On the other hand, he may ask for a cash sum for the chat, in which case put the phone down and find someone else to interview.

PREPARING YOURSELF

Preparing for the set piece interview

Time to get those reference books out and jump on the internet to find out as much as you can about the person in question. As you go through the information you've gathered, questions will pop into your mind that you think should have been asked at the time and missed. For example, if a player joined a club and left after a week and no reason was given, jot down a note to ask why. Sports stars seem more inclined to dish the dirt on a controversial incident once the dust has settled. It never ceases to amaze me how they are happy to wax lyrical about the event several months down the line after refusing to answer questions at the time. Be careful on personal matters, though, as the player may not want their life dragged through the mire. Would you like the failure of your marriage blasted across a paper in massive headlines?

Michael's advice

England striker Michael Owen is used to facing the press more than most since his meteoric rise to superstardom. But the down-to-earth Liverpool player is still willing to talk to the media as long as they leave his private life alone. He admitted:

> 'I have done a lot of interviews and I don't turn that many down even now. As long as you want to talk about football I don't think you will have many problems with people in the game. I have been in football long enough to know what I am going to be asked and if it is done in a polite manner I have no problems with journalists asking for interviews. But if you start asking questions about players' personal lives and things about my girlfriend, for instance, then I will refuse to answer.'

Preparing for the cold calling interview

This sort of interview is much more off the cuff and any background knowledge you have may come in handy. Quite often you will be trying to grab the scorer of the winning goal for a match report or a player set to come up against his former team or his toughest opponent for a preview piece. If you want to ask about a controversial point in a game just gone or a situation currently on-going, never jump in with it as your first question. Build up to it first with a series of softeners just to get your subject talking, otherwise he will clam up straight away. In these cases there are a stock list of questions worth remembering. Just avoid the obvious, as questions like 'did you think you would win?' will do you no favours. Memorise some of the stock questions below, as they will help get a conversation flowing.

For previews
- Who is the opponent's dangerman?
- Any old friends you are looking forward to playing against?
- Is it the first time you have played them since you left?
- Have you beaten this opponent before?

Post match
- What's the atmopshere in the dressing room like?
- What did the manager say?
- Did you enjoy that?
- It was a cracking goal, wasn't it?

Simon Mullock believes it is vitally important to get a sportsperson talking before firing your most important question at them as that way you will get the answer you are looking for. He adds:

> 'Build up your conversation with simple questions like asking how the season is going for them in particular. But I make sure I get them talkative before I ask a question that they may not want to answer. I always leave any tricky questions until the end in case I get short shrift from them. At least if they walk away at that point I have enough quotes to write a piece about them.'

KEEPING COOL

When I'm about to start an interview I find my stomach turning over in nervous excitement as though I was heading out on a first date. Questions flood my mind, such as what happens if they do not want to speak to me, or what if they refuse to answer my best questions? I'm sure you will go through the same traumas as well, but while the butterflies are good do not get over-anxious about a star's reactions. Just like the rest of the population there is one thing they are happier to talk about more than anything else in the world – themselves.

Don't be a robot
As you stand toe to toe with a star name it is easy to lose your cool and blurt out a bunch of inane questions which will leave you feel-

ing stupid and with nothing to write about. Although the primed questions above will get your subject talking, it can help to have a list of pre-thought out questions about a particular topic handy to stop yourself from becoming tongue tied at the vital moment.

If you do use a list, though, make sure you do not follow it parrot fashion and miss something important. If the star tells you he has had a big bust up and is walking out on the club, you will look pretty silly asking him whether he thinks he will reach his goal tally for the season. While having a list, I also listen carefully to what my interviewee is saying and if an answer leads off on a different tangent to the one I originally planned to follow, I let the conversation go down that route. Many times I have got a better piece than the one I intended to write by using this technique. I found a fact I did not know or heard a controversial view I was surprised to hear the player held.

Asking the obvious

How many times have you been told 'if you don't ask, you don't get'? The same principle applies to interviewing people, either because they do not know what it is you want or they refuse to tell you anything above the norm unless asked. So it does not matter how obvious the question is or the number of times it has been asked, make sure you put the point to your interviewee. I recently spent 20 minutes on the phone to a football manager talking about his team and his plans but never once asked him if he had signed a new player. When I picked up the paper the following morning I found to my cost someone else had asked him.

Winding up the interview

Once you've got all you need, it is time to wrap up the interview. In many cases this may be done for you by the sportsperson insisting they have to go, quite often before you have asked your main question. If you get the chance to have a civil ending make sure you thank the interviewee for chatting and if possible give them a business card. When doing this tell them if they see something about them with your name on they don't like they should get in touch. This ensures they look at your card and reinforces your name in their mind, which will come in useful when you meet again.

AVOIDING THE PITFALLS

So far grabbing an interview sounds like a walk in the park, but believe me it is far from it. You can spend the best part of an afternoon waiting for someone only for them to come out and decline a chat. Or you can spend a long time talking to a canny subject only for them not to divulge any of the things you want to know. You will also get used to other players interrupting your chat with rude shouts aimed at your subject that can break up your flow. There is no answer to these problems except just get on with it and do the best you can.

'I don't want to be here'

Another problem you will encounter is the star who just doesn't want to talk. There are times when a PR company has arranged an interview for you with a big name star and when you arrive it is obvious they do not want to be there. Remain friendly and charming and don't get abusive. Try out a few well-researched questions to make your subject think and gain his interest, but if none of these work plug on regardless and do the best you can. It can happen at any level as Nigel Matheson of *Match of the Day* magazine found out when he was sent to interview an uninterested David May of Manchester United (see Figure 11). You can almost imagine the painful silences and hear the desperation in Nigel's voice as an unhelpful May does his best to ruin what should have been a cover feature.

IMPROVING YOUR TECHNIQUE

Just like with your writing, the more practice you put in the better you will get at interviewing people. Before you even start to set up your first interview try out a few dummy runs with your friends and family. Let them pretend to be their favourite sports star and answer your questions. Not only will it be great fun for them, but also you will learn how to keep an interview flowing. Once you have a few of these dummy interviews on tape sit back and listen to your own voice and check for the following points:

- Do you interrupt too often?

- Do you sound rude?

- Is your questioning technique agonisingly slow?

- Have you missed an opportunity to ask an important question?

Listen carefully and compare your style to the way television and radio journalists interrogate their interviewees. Would you be frustrated if someone interviewed you with your style?

MOTD: Who is the greatest player you've been on the same pitch with?

DM: [Without looking up] Eric.

MOTD: What did you wear to Ryan Giggs' famous housewarming party, where the United players all went along in drag? Nicky Butt wore Laura Ashley apparently...

DM: I don't know what you're talking about. Nah, I didn't go.

MOTD: Weren't you invited?

DM: [Unconvincingly] No...

MOTD: Have you read *Addicted* by Tony Adams?

DM: I'm halfway through it right now. It's interesting, very interesting. I like the way it is so frank. No, I don't think there's any reason he should hold back.

MOTD: What do you remember from it?

DM: He drank quite a lot. He's also come out a better person for it.

MOTD: Worst room-mate in football?

DM: Pally. I can't say anything about his habits – too vulgar!

MOTD: Does Alex Ferguson send everyone in the squad a Christmas card?

DM: [Definitely] Yes, he does.

MOTD: Do you send one back, or don't you bother?

DM: Nah, we don't, no...

MOTD: If the United squad did *A Christmas Carol,* who would play Scrooge?

Phil Neville: [Suddenly taking an interest]
Chris Casper...

MOTD: And Tiny Tim?

DM: It would have been Pally but he's gone... [Laughs all round]

MOTD: Who is the funniest person in the Man United dressing room?

DM: I couldn't say.

Phil Neville: [Straight-faced] It's a laugh a minute in our dressing room.

MOTD: Best Christmas present you've ever had?

DM: Scalextric when I was eight or nine.

Fig. 11. The star who doesn't want to talk – David May's interview with *Match of the Day* magazine.

Questions to avoid

While some questions are great to get an interviewee talking, there are a few prickly points that could terminate an interview immediately. Enquire about the wrong thing and you will see your target marching towards their car at double pace, leaving you with your tape rolling and your ego deflated.

It's best *not* to ask:

- Is the manager really sleeping with your wife?

- Why are you not as good as you used to be?

- Is that talented youngster going to take your place in the team?

- Did you try and break your opponent's leg?

- How much do you hate your doubles partner?

MAKING IT EASY FOR YOURSELF

Having got your hot story on tape, it will be hard to contain yourself as you bash it out to sell for a fortune, but your excitement is sure to be dulled a little by the thought of having to listen to the interview and laboriously write down every sentence uttered by the interviewee. Believe me it is a long hard slog, but there is a technique which will allow you to cut through the drivel and rattle out your exclusive in double quick time. Use the tape counter on your dictaphone to help you. I keep a notepad open as I tape an interview and whenever I hear an important point I write down the counter number in my pad and jot alongside a brief note of the statement. When I come to write up the vital quotes I can then jump from point to point on the tape without having to go through the whole script. See Figure 12 for a picture of the technique.

CASE STUDIES

A big snub for Andy

Spurred on by seeing his piece in the national paper, Andy decides it is time to join in with the big boys and seek out a star name to interview. He tracks down his man and even convinces him to stop for a chat, but annoyed by his aggressive line of questioning the sportsman tells Andy he has to rush and a great opportunity is wasted.

Fig. 12. Using a tape counter.

Jane's got it taped

Despite learning shorthand at school, Jane is finding it hard to keep pace with writing down the answers and coming up with fresh questions to stop the interview falling flat. She invests in a dictaphone. The move pays dividends as she feels more in control when interviewing and finds the quotes she types up from her tape recorder help improve the articles she is producing.

CHECKLIST

1. What should you wear when you interview a star?

2. Interview a family member and observe your body language while you are chatting.

3. What are the two ways to set up an interview?

4. Set up a pretend interview with a star and write out a list of questions.

5. Tape yourself interviewing someone and listen to the tape carefully.

6. Write down five questions you would not want to be asked and remember them.

10

Maximising Your Earning Potential

SELLING ONE STORY TO MORE THAN ONE PUBLICATION

When I first started out freelancing my biggest concern was having to rewrite the same story five different ways so that each national paper had their own version. I need not have bothered as I soon discovered by reading through the papers they were happy to take a story that had been given to every paper. They either rejigged it into their style or in many cases just ran the story as it was written.

Selling to a wider audience is a different tale altogether, though, with a need for plenty of decorum and common sense. If you start talking to two magazines about the same story and they both want it you could land yourself in trouble. Even if you use a completely different angle for each magazine it will not take long for them to guess you have done both pieces and once they work that out you won't work for them again.

But if the story you have is right for a magazine as well as a newspaper try and sell it to both. Be aware that the magazine will not want the same line that has appeared in national papers as by the time they go to print it will be old hat. If it has only appeared in a regional paper, though, they are unlikely to be aware of the tale and will be interested.

PICKING UP MORE THAN ONE STORY FROM AN INTERVIEW

This is where a good freelance really comes into their own. As you listen to what the interviewee is saying, continuously think in your head of which publication would be interested in what they have just said. To do this successfully it is important to know your markets well. For example, if you are previewing a rugby league game between St Helens and Leeds with a Rhinos' player and he waxes lyrical about the Saints' star player it is worth contacting the local Liverpool press to see if they are interested in taking a piece. If he then goes on to criticise a ban he has just received, the national papers and the rugby league press may be interested in the tale. In effect, whenever you interview someone always keep your mind open for the possibilities. If you go thinking you will make just one pay packet out of the interview, one pay packet is all you will make.

Try to:

* Arrive for the interview with more than one idea in your head.

* Think about which titles may take a piece before you set off.

* Get the sports star talking about several topics.

* Mention the biggest issue of the day in case the interviewee has a strong view.

BEWARE OF OTHER JOURNALISTS

As we have already discussed, your role as a freelance means your presence is often looked upon with suspicion by staff writers who are worried the story you have could be better than the one they hold.

They are also fearful that you may have got the same story as them and are about to sell it to all their rivals before their paper has a chance to give it a show. You can understand their worries as they will no doubt get an angry reaction from their boss if other papers scoop them all the time. You can, of course, take great delight in showing the staff writer how much better than them you are, but I would not recommend it. You will find life a lot easier with the staff writer on your side rather than against you.

Try and build up a working relationship where you discuss the story you have and what plans you have for it. You may find that every now and then you have to lose out on a story to keep the staff writer happy, but as long as they will help you in return then it is worth losing a little cash in the short term to make more in the long run.

SAVING UP FOR A RAINY DAY

Sometimes it pays to box clever and owning a decent radio can also help. Quite often you may have a story that will 'hold' – a tale no one will use straight away. If you find that on the day you've picked up the tale there are several other big stories happening it is worth waiting before approaching papers. For example, the day a local club goes into receivership or leading up to an important World Cup qualifier is not the best time to punt around your tale of an 18-year-old winning a player of the season award. Wait until the dust settles before getting on the phone.

PICKING UP STORIES OTHERS MISS

There are two ways to do this and both mean you having to go the extra mile in your search for success. The most common way is to wait and wait and wait in the freezing cold for the key person of your story to appear after a game, meeting or training session. 'All good things come to those who wait' in the perfect world, but not in the sports world. If you are prepared to wait longer than anyone else you may get the exclusive your patience deserves or you could get told to go away.

The other way is to listen more intently than others when you are doing group interviews and if you see an angle the others have missed keep your mouth closed. Once the interview is over follow the interviewee away from the group and throw in a supplementary question. Probably the best example of this is the TV detective Columbo, who used to finish his interview and then just pop back with one last key question that always hit the honey pot.

USING YOUR CUTTINGS TO FIND MORE WORK

What do you do once you finish writing a story and send it off to the relevant publication? Do you throw the typed sheet in the bin or delete the file from the computer to save space in your memory? If you do you may be throwing away money.

I keep everything I write as well as cutting out and filing every magazine or newspaper article that may come in useful in the future. It will astound you the amount of times you search for some old quotes in a bid to spice up or pad out a new piece. In a few cases you may even have some quotes you never used that are suddenly just right to exploit the latest issue in the sport you cover. Maybe the local hockey league wants to change the format of the cup. If you already have in your notepad a respected figure's words about how much he or she loves a cup run you are only a short step away from making some money.

THE SALES FUNNEL

Have you ever heard of a top salesman who never leaves his office and does without a phone? No? That is not surprising as the only way his product will sell is if he keeps telling people how good it is. Selling your skills as a reporter is no different. If you do not tell desks you are available for work and can do a good job for them they will never offer you work. You have to be prepared to contact a lot of people for just a little success in the sports writing game. But when you do talk to people don't over-do the sales pitch as this will undoubtedly put them off. Look at the sales funnel in Figure 13. Pop in ten leads at the top and one potential sale will pop out of the bottom. It does not always work to that percentage but it is not far off. So as you can see you need to do a lot of writing and ringing before you find regular customers and it is important the early rejections do not put you off.

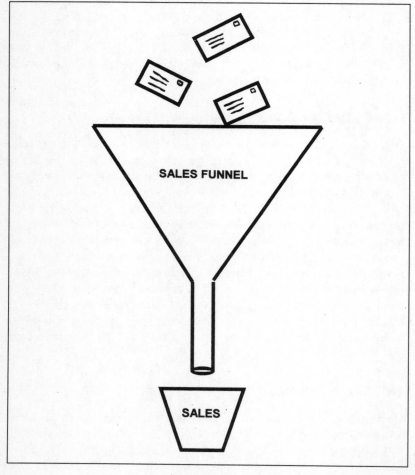

SALES FUNNEL

SALES

Fig. 13. The sales funnel.

CASE STUDIES

The cash tills are ringing for Andy

Unperturbed by his recent unsuccessful brush with sports stars, Andy visits a local training ground and speaks to the manager about his plans for the club. The manager is in a good mood and is unusually forthcoming, telling Andy about his latest transfer target. Just for good measure he blasts one of his rival clubs for trying to poach his star youth team captain. Andy gets home and realises he has struck gold and manages to sell stories to four different regional papers and a short piece to a couple of national papers.

Clever Jane

While attending another squash tournament for a national paper Jane grabs an interview with one of the star players. He attacks the governing body, claims a young player at his club is going to be a superstar and adds he is considering playing on for ten more years. Jane is sharp enough to realise she has a good chance to make some money and sells the governing body story to the national paper as a follow-up. She also agrees a price with the local paper on the squash player named as a potential superstar and manages to use the rest in a magazine feature.

CHECKLIST

1. Is it okay to sell your story to more than one publication?

2. Interview a friend and see how many different stories you can pick up in one go.

3. Why is it important to keep hold of your cuttings?

4. For what reason should you not hold back a story?

5. Who is it important not to upset?

11

Keeping on the Right Side of the Law

SAVING YOURSELF FROM A LAW SUIT

There is an old saying that 'the pen is mightier than the sword'. As the wielder of words you must realise how the power you hold can hurt people and also damage you at the same time. In this chapter we will look at the law and how it will affect you in your everyday work as a freelancer.

UNDERSTANDING THE LAW OF LIBEL

Committing libel is one of the biggest sins for a journalist and also one of the most expensive. It can prove so costly that all news organisations have their own lawyer who spends his or her time deciding whether a contentious piece can be printed without fear of a law suit. Even then the experts can get it wrong as proved by the award of £1 million to Elton John some years back over a libellous piece in a tabloid.

What is libel?

We are lucky in Great Britain that we enjoy free speech, but that can be abused with the media sometimes over-stepping the mark and producing pieces that can be painful and damage the career of professional people. It is an amazing truth that once a fact appears in print people believe it, however absurd it may sound. Even if the fact is wrong and is proved to be so, there is always talk of there being 'no smoke without fire'. Imagine how frustrating it would be if it was you that had been burnt at the stake.

To prevent this happening, laws were introduced to stop the media committing libel or slander. The difference between the two is that **libel** is a defamatory statement in a written form while **slander** is in a verbal form. Both have to be seen or heard by a third person before libel can be proved.

A **defamatory statement** is one that:

* exposes the target to ridicule, hatred or contempt

- causes them to be shunned or avoided

- lowers their reputation in the minds of right-minded people

- disparages them in their business or profession.

Of course, all the above are open to interpretation and that is left up to the judge who will advise a jury on whether the statement could have been defamatory. The jury then have to decide whether the plaintiff was actually defamed.

Close to the knuckle
In sport the lines drawn up by libel law are nearly transgressed every day. For example, calling former England manager Graham Taylor a turnip head after a defeat could be considered as lowering his reputation and disparaging him. The tabloids got away with that one and even when claims of match-fixing in football sprang to light recently and the accused were proved not guilty the paper who ran the story still walked off without facing any libel action.

The ins and outs of innuendo
Just because you do not actually name someone you can still face a libel action if the courts believe there was innuendo in your article. If the plaintiff can prove that despite not being named, people can still work out from the article who they are, then they have a case.

The defences against libel
There are many defences to a libel case but the most frequently used one in sporting circles is without a doubt 'fair comment'. Calling someone a bad manager could be construed as disparaging them in their profession, but if the manager in question has lost six out of six league games then you could easily argue your statement was simply *fair comment*.

Other defences are:

- *justification* – you can prove every point in your story to be true

- *privilege* – this protects statements made in court and Parliament

- *unintentional defamation* – the libel was made accidentally and without knowledge that the statement was defamatory.

Protecting yourself against libel
There is only one sure way to safeguard against libelling someone – do not write anything contentious. If the whole story is close to the

mark, check your facts three times and if one of the points fails to measure up either leave it alone or talk to the desk of whichever paper you intend to sell it to. They may take it as a tip-off and investigate the story themselves. If it ends up in print you will be paid a tip-off fee and have saved yourself from facing a potentially expensive lawsuit. If they do not take up the story I would suggest you spike it rather than take a risk a newspaper is not prepared to take.

Never repeat a libel
Do not fall into the trap of believing it is safe to use a libellous quote because it has already appeared once in print. The complainant can sue every time it is repeated, and it is not only you that will be sued. They can also start legal action against the sub-editor, the editor and the publisher – a sure way to nip your career in the bud.

KNOWING ABOUT COPYRIGHT AND WHO OWNS IT

While it is very important not to commit libel, it is just as important not to breach someone's copyright. The most recent copyright law was passed in 1988 under the title of the Copyright, Designs and Patents Act. The Act was passed to protect writers, publications and artists from having their hard work exploited by other media organisations.

What is copyright?
Copyright does not cover facts and ideas, simply the way you put the facts to use. For example, if a paper runs a story about a player signing a new five-year contract one day after its rival there is no copyright breach as long as they report the fact using different words. But if you see a story in a magazine and then sell the story with the same quotes to a newspaper you are in breach of the magazine's copyright. Similarly, if you write a feature about five former players talking about their best moment in sport and another magazine runs a piece with five different players talking about the same topic there is no copyright breach.

Who owns the copyright?
This is probably one of the most important pieces of information for a freelance to remember. When you submit work as a freelance the copyright for the work is owned by you. Even if the work has been ordered from you or used by a publication, you keep the copyright. Only if you agree to sign your rights over to the publication, which

some magazines and on the odd occasion newspapers ask you to do, will you lose the copyright.

Borrowing quotes from other media

Media such as books, plays and television programmes are all subject to copyright because they are an original product. But under certain circumstances you can take quotes from them as long as certain rules are followed – this is called 'fair dealing'. Taking soundbites from other media sources and crediting where the quote came from is now widely accepted in the industry.

For example, it is okay to write: 'I want to stay at this club for as long as I can,' Peter Smith told Clubcall.

However, lifting large segments of quotes even with a credit is not a wise thing to do. It can not only land you in trouble but also upset other journalists you need to work with in future. They will not take kindly to you making money from their endeavours. If you don't have the quotes to write the piece it is sometimes better to just leave well alone.

CASE STUDIES

Andy is saved by the bell

After covering a particularly stormy game for his local paper Andy speaks to one of the players about the referee. The player calls the referee a cheat and adds he thinks he takes bribes. Andy is keen to get his exclusive in that night's special sports paper but a call on his mobile forces him to rewrite his match report and the chance is missed. It is a lucky break for Andy as the story is libellous and if he had filed the tale it could have landed him in trouble.

Jane is a credit to the copyright laws

A few days after interviewing a local cricket player Jane spots a piece about him in the local paper with some interesting quotes on areas she failed to ask about. Rather than send a second-rate piece of work to the magazine that commissioned her she cleverly points out the topic in her piece and adds some spice to it by using the quotes. She hands herself a way out of trouble by crediting the local paper in her article for the quotes she used.

CHECKLIST

1. What is the libel law and why shouldn't you break it?

2. What is a defamatory statement?

3. What are the defences against a defamatory statement?

4. How can you protect yourself against libel?

5. Visit your library and find a book about the libel laws and those that have broken them.

6. Who owns the copyright to your work?

7. Can you use quotes that have been in other publications?

12

Accounting and the Taxman

HAVING A HEAD FOR FIGURES

Unfortunately for every bit of pleasure there has to come a little pain and in sports writing that comes with the mass of paperwork needed to ensure you and, of course, the taxman gets paid. While it is fun charging off left, right and centre to watch your favourite sports for free and a big boost to your ego to see your name in print, do not forget there will be hours of tedium and boredom. These teeth grindingly, frustrating moments will be typing numbers into a spreadsheet or number crunching with accounting books, but if you want to get paid it is a necessary evil.

KEEPING RECORDS

There is a simple rule when it comes to working out what information you have to keep for the taxman – **note down everything**. Once you've finished this book dash out to the shops and buy several lined cashbooks and a dozen pens and don't forget to pick up the receipt. By the way did you keep your receipt for this book? You need to ask for a receipt for everything you buy and keep them in dated order.

Personally I have an old shoebox which has envelopes for each of the categories listed below with receipts bulging out of each of them. I have found my record-keeping has got easier since I decided to break down my accounts into the following categories and tot up the totals once a month.

- newspapers

- travel

- office equipment

- stationery

- sustenance

- books.

The reason it is so important to keep these records is so you can claim it against tax. Now I can guess the next question on your lips – what exactly can you claim? The answer is simple; anything you spend that is for sole use in your work as a freelance. For example, petrol used driving to a football game you are covering is claimable. Petrol used on the way to your mum's for Sunday lunch, when you stopped off to buy a magazine you need, is not.

ACCOUNTING METHODS

Computer software

Whether you want to keep your records on computer or by using a series of accounting books is totally up to you. It doesn't matter how you do it as long as you do. I personally use Sage's Instant Accounting package, which is simple to operate and has the added advantage of being the same software as my accountant uses. I input all my invoices, payments and purchase records and at a touch of a button it produces a whole host of information. It can churn out my company profit or a comparison of the amount I have spent on petrol in relation to the previous year to help me review my budgets.

Pen and paper

If you do not own a computer or prefer to work out your figures by hand there are plenty of tools to help. Explaining what to do in every instance would take too long here so pick up a good accountancy book from your local bookshop. To find the right type of accounting books necessary to start keeping records, pop along to your local stationers and gaze through the numerous types on display. Alternatively if you have been in contact with a local enterprise agency to ask for help in setting up as a freelance, write to the address below and ask for a free set of books:

George Vyner Ltd, PO Box 1, Holmfirth, Huddersfield HD7 2RP. Tel: (01484) 685221.

BANKING AND INVOICING

Bank accounts

Opening up a new bank account for your freelance work is a good idea, but only if you intend to make a few pennies from your scribblings. If you are in the game for fun there is no need, but if you are serious about making a living from writing or supplementing your income an account will make life easier. I would suggest looking at a charge-free building society account or one of the new supermarket accounts with a good rate of interest. These allow you to take out cash when you need it but will also pay your interest on the sum you will inevitably have to set aside for the taxman. Another advantage of having a separate bank account is the ever-increasing number of publications that use the BACS system where money is paid straight into your bank account and a remittance slip detailing the payment is sent to you.

Sending out invoices

This is one of the most important parts of making a living out of sports writing because if you don't send out invoices you will not get paid. You can make your invoice as simple or as fancy as you want it (check out the example in Figure 14), but it has to include the following:

JOHN FREDICKS
45 Ashworth Drive
Oxtown
OD7 8EF
Tel: (01797 563647)

January 5 199X

Oxdown Times
29 Barnsby Street
Oxdown
OD2 7JD

Dear Ian,

I would be grateful if you could pass the following invoice for me:

INVOICE

December 12	Sarah set to be a star	£25.00
December 16	Ashworth Town v Filingborough	£30.00
December 20	Squash press conference	£25.00
		———
Total		£80.00

Fig. 14. Example of an invoice.

- your name and address
- the piece of work you are claiming payment for
- the publication date
- if a sum has been agreed, add this, *or*
- include the date, story headline and the page it was on.

The completed invoice should be sent to the person who ordered the work who will sign it off for payment by the accounts department and hopefully a cheque will soon be in the post.

Chasing invoices

In an ideal world you will fire off five invoices and three days later five cheques will land on your doormat. Sports journalism is not an ideal world. Note down every piece of work of yours that appears in print and every order you receive a commission for, with the name of the person who asked for the work. Some companies operate a self-billing system where they calculate the work you do for them and pay accordingly, but I have found these systems to be far from foolproof. If a company tells you not to bother because they log everything at their end, ignore them and write down all the work you do for them as I guarantee the odd piece will be missing from the remittance slip. When the payment slip does arrive check it against your list because there are invariably mistakes.

To ensure prompt payment, make sure you:

- send your invoices at the earliest opportunity
- chase your accounts
- mark on the invoices that you expect payment within 30 days
- be polite when asking why your cheque has not arrived.

It is not a good idea to shout abuse at the first person that answers the phone as the contributor payment department can only pay out what they have been told to by the sports desk. You may well have to go back to the desk and check what has been sent through for payment. However frustrating this is, always keep your cool because there will only be one loser if you blow your top and that will be YOU.

Paying invoices

Despite being classified as a small business I like to take the lead of major corporations when it comes to paying invoices sent to me in that I pay only on the red bill. There are, of course, exceptions to the rule and I mainly make these when it comes to someone who has been particularly helpful or anyone who undertakes freelance work for me. For bigger bills like the telephone I tend to wait for the red bill and then ask if I can split the payment over two months. As long as you have not missed a payment before I have found major companies happy to accommodate and this method also helps with your cash flow.

COMPLETING YOUR TAX RETURN

Paying tax is a painful experience but all of us have to go through it, I'm afraid. Trying to avoid it may bring success for a short time but do not ever believe you have got away without paying your tax as the Inland Revenue has a habit of catching up with you. Even if you decide not to inform them of your extra income they will soon be in touch courtesy of the invoices you have sent out. When they check through your customer's accounts they will spot your name and if you have not informed them of your work, will kindly send you a tax return in the post.

Working out how much you owe

I am lucky that my business has a big enough turnover to support the need for an accountant. But I still make sure that my records are kept in the best order I can so that I only pay my accountant for calculating my tax return and not for spending hours trying to sift through my poorly kept paperwork. If your turnover does not warrant an accountant I suggest you look at some of the latest computer programs on the market that can help work out your tax bill. I have in the past used the Which Tax software, which I found helpful. I simply inputted the numbers requested and it printed out a fully completed return form for me.

CASE STUDIES

Tax fate is sealed for Andy

The thought of sitting at home sorting out receipts rather than being in the field chasing stories is frustrating Andy so he sorts out his own accounting device. He buys ten A4 envelopes and separates his receipts into certain categories. From now on when he empties his pockets he puts each receipt in the appropriate envelope and plans to sort them all out at the end of the tax year.

Money worries for Jane

Jane's patience snaps when after two months she has yet to receive a penny from a magazine she does regular work for. She phones their accounts department and they have no record of her invoice. A call to the editor reveals her PA has been on sick leave for a month and no processing has taken place. Her call prompts the editor into action and she promises to pay Jane straight away if she sends another invoice.

CHECKLIST

1. What receipts should you keep and why?

2. Take a trip to your local computer software shop and check out the accounting packages.

3. Are you doing enough work to contemplate a second bank account?

4. Draw up an invoice in your style, making sure your name and address are prominent.

5. How long should you wait before chasing an invoice?

13

Working From Home

When starting up as a freelance I doubt you will be moving into top-notch offices in the centre of town next to the best coffee shop in the area. In fact my guess is you will probably be crammed into the spare bedroom or working from the dining table, picking up your paperwork whenever a mealtime arrives. So here are a few tips to help ease problems at home.

CONSIDERING YOUR PERSONAL RELATIONSHIPS

'My wife says it would be better if there was another woman, at least then she would know what she is up against. But she says, "How can I compete against football?" '

Don Mackay, former Blackburn manager

How you are going to get on with your partner or the rest of the family is probably the one thing you will overlook in the rush to decide where to put your shiny new printer. But it is *the* most important point to look into before charging headfirst into freelance work. You can have the best writing style in Wapping but if your partner is resentful about the way your work has taken over the house, churning out wonderful pieces on Britain's next high-jump champion will not make you happy.

I would advise before you start out on the freelance trail that you discuss with everyone in your household the changes freelancing will make in your life. Make sure they appreciate that you will:

• work more evenings and weekends than before

• have times when you need peace and quiet

• take up more space and become a nuisance

• get frustrated by a lack of success.

Talk about how this will affect your living environment and your relationships and remember to listen as well. You will need to make some concessions even though you will be reluctant to do so. Include everyone who lives in your home in any decision-making process. By letting them help in the littlest things, like devising a workspace plan for your equipment, they will be more inclined to take an interest in your dream and give you more backing than you would otherwise have enjoyed.

SORTING OUT YOUR WORKSPACE

This is a crucial decision as setting up your workspace is the foundation on which your success will be built. Working in the hallway by the toilet is not going to be conducive to writing your next masterpiece, neither will cramming yourself into a spare room where you trip over your chair every time you reach for a book. Start by making a list of all the things you will be doing and the equipment you need. For example:

- using the phone
- writing notes
- typing into a computer
- printing off invoices
- reading books
- a quiet area.

Now walk around the house and find the best place to base yourself for all your needs. Don't forget it is easier to bring Mohammed to the mountain than the other way around. So remember if everything is right for you to work in the dining room but the vital phone point is missing, it may be easier to put in a second junction box rather than squeeze into a corner of the living room.

Keeping it safe

As well as making yourself comfortable you also need to consider the safety implications of where you intend to work. Is your chair going to trip up someone on his or her way to the toilet? Will there be enough light so you don't damage your eyes? Or are you so crammed up that any paperwork will swamp you and leave you frustrated as you spend an age searching for that important note you made yesterday?

Laying out your office

Once you have decided where you intend to base yourself resist the temptation to pile in and start building your desk and unpacking your computer kit. Take a step back and think for 24 hours. You guessed it; it's time for a list to be made. Write down on a sheet of paper everything you intend to put in your office and once you've finished rewrite the list in order of usage with the most important objects at the top. Now you know which articles to consider putting in the most convenient places and what will have to go in the space left over.

Mapping out your office

Armed with your list draw a quick map of where everything must go in your office space to make it most comfortable. Obviously the computer has to go on the desk, but use a bit of lateral thinking about other items. Take a trip to an office equipment firm and a furniture superstore like B&Q or IKEA and look for ingenious space-saving devices to store paperwork and books. If you have space pick up a second-hand filing cabinet or if you are not blessed with enough room try a smaller cardboard one. Once you have found everything you need, it is time to start building your workspace.

THE INSURANCE DILEMMA

If you only plan to cover the odd game for your local paper, or run off 15 paragraphs of weekly copy about the local sailing regatta, there is no need to investigate the numerous types of insurance available for people working from home. But if you intend to run your own freelance empire from your spare bedroom there are a few facts you should look at and unfortunately they will cost you money.

Insurance is the one thing that is always left until last but if you plan to make a serious go of your business do not shelve your insurance plans. You must:

- tell your insurance company you are working from home
- check out professional indemnity insurance
- look at public liability insurance
- change your car insurance.

Working from home is sure to increase your premium but it is better to pay a bit more now than lose a lot more later if your home is broken into. The same applies with your car as driving to sports events on a regular basis is sure to mean you need business cover.

The good news is that professional indemnity and public liability are two types of insurance you can probably do without. Professional indemnity covers you against action when a client uses your advice and comes to harm in doing so. In our trade it is hard to think of any advice you will give out that may lead to a claim. Public liability is needed to protect yourself if customers or staff are injured while working in your house. Before signing up for the insurance it's worth asking yourself it customers are going to visit you and if they are not, think twice. But if you are at all worried, sign up as it's better to be safe than sorry.

If you have any doubts about which kind of insurance you need, contact a local registered insurance broker.

CASE STUDIES

Space is tight for Andy

The lack of a regular income has forced Andy to start up his fledgling freelance career from his bedroom, but with every new book or magazine he buys the space he has to work in shrinks. Finally he decides the cramped conditions are affecting his work and he spends his first pay cheque on a workstation allowing him to reorganise his bedroom and giving him space to work in – for the time being.

A room with a view

Jane is luckier than Andy as her two-bedroom house gives her as much space as she needs. Just as importantly the wonderful view she enjoys from the window when she is working helps inspire her to carry on working when she feels like a break. The chance to pop downstairs and make a coffee and then spend a few minutes watching the birds dance among the trees lifts her enough to return to work.

CHECKLIST

1. Who are the most important people to consider when you work from home?

2. What should you explain to members of your household before starting working from home?

3. Write a list of articles you need to work from home successfully.

4. Draw a map of your office including the items from the list above.

5. Contact your insurance broker to check what cover you need.

14

Getting Motivated

BE READY TO SWEAT FOR SUCCESS

There is an old saying that success is 10 per cent inspiration and 90 per cent perspiration, but it is a saying I only partly agree with. The wise old man who came up with this message aimed at ruining the dream of overnight stardom for a million people didn't go deep enough. I personally believe success is 100 per cent inspiration, because when you have perspired for so long without achieving anything you need the inspiration to keep going. But how do you find an endless stream of inspiration? It is simple, you need good self-motivation and discipline.

SETTING TARGETS

If you jumped onto a jet plane you would expect the pilot to know exactly where to go – otherwise you would never get there. But ask yourself now exactly what it is you want to achieve from being a free-lance writer and see if you can conjure up an answer. If you struggle then you are in real trouble because if you don't know what your personal destination is, how can you get there?

And it's not good enough just to say 'I want to write for my local newspaper' and leave it like that. You need to be more specific. When a lazy person decides to get in shape they generally make the mistake of saying they intend to get fit without drawing up the parameters they need to reach to know they are fit. Now if they said they wanted to be fit enough to run five miles three times a week they will find achieving their goal a whole lot easier.

- Start out with a goal and write it down.

- Work out how to measure when that goal will be reached.

- Plan a weekly structure which leads you to that goal.

- Once you have reached the goal set a new one.

- Stay flexible. If the first deadline is missed, set another target.

It is important to continuously re-examine your goals because once you have reached one you will find yourself heading nowhere until you set a new one.

Achieving your objectives

With your goals clearly outlined you can feel comfortable knowing your career has a structure. Now you have to guide yourself on a daily basis to reach your targets. Start by making the following:

- a daily list
- a weekly list
- a short-term list
- a long-term list.

Start with the long-term list, which should cover the next five years of your life. Include on it who you want to be writing for at that point in your life. Do not be shy – as the list is personal, put on it every-thing you want to achieve. Then think about each item and work out how it will be achieved and what the first steps on the road to meet-ing your goals are. This information makes up your short-term list. This should be aimed at things you intend to happen in the first year. From today begin to make a weekly list of objectives that need to be reached if your twelve-month goal is to be achieved and do this every week for the rest of your life. Once again break this down into a daily category and assign a time during each day for carrying out the task.

Using the daily list

This is not the most important list to make as without the long-term goals there will be nothing to put on the daily list, but it is helpful in ensuring you maintain discipline and get your work done in time. Each morning add your daily jobs to any items already written down from the weekly list of tasks you have outlined for today and give them a number in order of importance (see Figure 15). Then rewrite the list in number order and pin it somewhere prominent. As your day progresses check off each item as you complete the task until you have finished every job on the list – it does happen on rare occa-sions. If for some reason it is impossible to execute a task, move on to the next one, but keep coming back to the most significant task before taking a further step down the daily list. If, as will be the most frequent occurrence, there are jobs left over, add them to tomorrow's list.

Long-term goals:

- Earn £2,000 a week
- Have three holidays a year
- Own four-bedroom house
- Write a feature for a broadsheet every week
- Have own magazine column
- Be friends with a top sports star
- Cover a top football match every week

Short-term goals:

- Earn £750 a week
- Have one British and one foreign holiday a year
- Buy two-bedroom house
- Write a feature for any publication per month
- Have a piece in every magazine I want to write for
- Have occasional drinks with sports stars
- Cover a football match a week

Weekly list

- Earn £750
- Save for holidays
- Put money aside for mortgage
- Think up and try and sell five-feature ideas
- Write to one magazine about column
- Set up a drink with a sports star
- Phone around for matches
- Write to five potential customers

Daily list

- Phone local manager to ask about possible signings
- Write up story from notebook
- Read two magazine features
- Think up a magazine idea
- Phone paper to ask for a match to cover
- Go to bank
- Write to at least one potential customer

Fig. 15. Listing your goals and tasks.

COPING WITH STRESS

Journalism is one of the most stressful businesses to be involved in as few other professions have so many deadlines every day. People who work in the industry are always being pushed to reach the next deadline and once that has been achieved there is another one to look forward to. It is a hard life with long unsociable hours, little job security and very little of the glamour people associate with the trade. Stress is rife and leads to many heart attacks and nervous breakdowns so do not expect any sports desk to feel sorry for you when you hit high stress levels – and believe me you will.

It is probable that you are planning to start freelance sports writing as a sideline while you continue your career and that will mean you are putting yourself under extra stress. Days will be spent rushing from your office to a match without time for tea and then a late night will follow before you wake tired in the morning and head for the office again. So first you need to recognise when you are under stress. Look for the following symptoms:

- you become sulky

- you smoke and drink more

- your neck feels tense

- you have headaches

- your eyes become red and bloodshot.

Alleviating stress

There is only one way to deal with stress and that is to alleviate the problem because if you let it carry on, the pressure will only get worse. The best way to ease the stress is to organise your day in a better way to ensure you get as much done as possible in a short space of time. We will touch on other ideas later that include:

- raising your self-esteem

- making quick decisions

- socialising with friends

- using your head

- taking time out to relax.

MANAGING YOUR TIME EFFECTIVELY

We have already looked at one aspect of this earlier in the chapter when we talked about making lists to ensure your day is well organised, but there are numerous other tips worth trying out:

- Set all clocks to the right time.

- Always leave extra time in case of a traffic build-up when you set off for appointments.

- Find a central place to leave important things like keys and wallets.

- Don't let the car run low on fuel and then waste time finding a garage.

KEEPING YOUR SELF-ESTEEM HIGH

It is human nature to wonder what friends, family, acquaintances and people you do not even know think about you. Most important, though, is what you think about yourself. If you think you have little chance of succeeding as a freelance sports reporter, you won't succeed. I play football on a Sunday and was once hugely frustrated by a young member of our team after I told him to take on the opponents' rather dodgy left-back. He replied 'But I won't be able to beat him,' and unsurprisingly he never did. If he had taken a different tack, though, and thought to himself, 'I can beat him. He looks a little slow,' I bet he would have enjoyed a whole lot more success and wouldn't have spent the last 30 minutes of the game watching from the bench after being substituted.

People you meet react to the way you are more than you would imagine. If they find you a confident person who appears to know where you are going in life they will be more inclined to help you get there than if they view you as a ditherer hoping to land on your feet somehow or other.

Raising your self-esteem

There used to be an old television advert that proclaimed 'feeling fit, looking good' and it is advice that is well heeded. Shake up your diet by buying a book on healthier eating and follow its guidelines. Try taking more exercise and drink and smoke less. This will help you look better and feel better about yourself. Dress positively by wearing clothes that are appropriate and reflect your personality. Buy a full-length mirror and try on all your clothes so you can see the 'whole you'. Any items that no longer suit you should be put into your car-cleaning clothes pile.

MAKING THE RIGHT DECISIONS

I find one of the most draining aspects of the freelance business is being unable to make a decision. I spend hours awake at night turning the options over in my mind and frustrate friends by ignoring them as the same questions keep exploding in my head. All of this raises my stress levels unnecessarily and adds a few more grey hairs to my already silver-tinted head. That was until recently when I realised that despite spending hours mulling over important decisions I nearly always went with the gut reaction I felt when the problem first arose. Now I spend less time worrying and more time achieving.

SOCIALISING WITH FRIENDS

When problems do arise and I can feel things start getting on top of me, I have a simple system of easing the strain – I phone a friend. Ten minutes of irrelevant chat and things don't seem so bad. At the same time I have kept in touch with a mate, so I can cross that off my list of things to do. Alternatively turn on the radio or television for five minutes and watch whatever you find – and with the quality of daytime TV you will soon find yourself desperate to return to work, but in a more relaxed manner.

USING YOUR HEAD

Stress comes from pressure you place on yourself to succeed and therefore you are the only person capable of easing your stress levels. Talk the pressure off by using self-talking techniques. Tell yourself:

- This job will be hard but I can do it.
- I'm nervous about this phone call but I've made harder ones before.
- The deadlines are tight but I thrive under pressure.
- This is my biggest interview but I'm only asking questions.

TAKING TIME OUT

In chasing your dream you need to be focused and have plenty of self-confidence and a willingness to work very hard. But sometimes too much hard work with very little play can be just as bad as no work at all. Stoke City manager Brian Little admits his time as boss at Aston Villa was not helped by his desire to succeed. He eventually quit the Villa job because he felt under too much pressure of his own making. When Little looks back he now acknowledges he was trying too hard and having the odd day off would have helped him take better stock of how to improve the club.

CASE STUDIES

Goal king Andy hits his targets
While Andy is not a great believer in writing down his goals on a checklist, he did know in his mind what he wanted to achieve. But once he reached his goal of making enough money to survive and selling an article to a national paper Andy became bored with his writing. Out of frustration he sits down and writes out a list of new goals to aim for and within days he is back to his bubbly best and determined to reach his targets again.

A list a day helps Jane work, rest and play
Jane's busy life and the endless rounds of homework to mark from her teaching job leave her with little time to write. But by jotting down weekly and daily lists she manages to keep her life under control and get nearly everything she plans for the week sorted out. She also has long-term goals pinned to a noticeboard and feels comfortable that despite the distractions she will succeed.

CHECKLIST

1. Write down a list of everything you want to achieve.

2. Break it down until you come up with a daily list.

3. What are the symptoms of stress?

4. What is the best way to rid yourself of stress?

5. What can you do to improve your time management?

6. Why is self-esteem important to the successful person?

Glossary

Agency. A company that writes and sells stories to publications. They have no publication of their own and have close ties with their regular customers.

Agents. Most sports stars now employ agents to look after their affairs. The agent negotiates contracts for the player and is often used as a buffer to stop the player having to speak to the press.

BACS. A payment system whereby newspapers can pay directly into your bank account rather than having to send you a cheque.

British Lions. A scratch rugby team using players from all four home nations which tours South Africa, Australia and New Zealand on a rota basis every four years.

CD-ROM. A round disk for computers, similar to the music-playing CDs, which can hold vast quantities of information and is used to load programs onto PCs.

Clubcall. A company that supplies the latest news and interviews from an individual sporting club on a premium price phone line.

Commission. When you are asked to cover an event or write a piece about a certain topic by a publication. Once you are commissioned you will be paid for your work even if it is not used.

Contacts book. A list of phone numbers of sports players who can be contacted to give quotes about a dilemma relating to them. The better your contacts book the further you will go as a journalist.

Copy. The story you file to a publication.

Copy-takers. Typists employed by newspapers to take your copy over the phone and send it to their desks.

Cover feature. A feature with a star who is big enough to have their picture put on the front of the magazine with the knowledge it will boost the publications sales.

English Cricket Board. The organisation which runs English cricket.

Feature. An in-depth interview which is written in a softer style than a straight news story.

Freelance. Any working journalist who does not have full-time employment with a newspaper or magazine.

Freephone numbers. 0800 numbers newspapers use to allow their correspondents to phone the desks and copy-takers without charge.

Headline. A phrase put on the top of copy to grab the reader's eye and entice them to take interest in the story.

Insurance broker. A salesman who can advise his customers about which types of insurance policies are on the market.

Intro. The first paragraph of a story. It should give the reader an idea of what the story is about as well as tempt them to read on.

ISP. Internet Service Provider. A company that allows you to log on to the internet through their gateway and download pages. The majority charge for this service.

Laptop. A portable personal computer which houses its own screen and can be used without the need of a power cable.

Match order. The specifications of time and length that a paper asks for when they order a match report from a freelance.

NCTJ. National Council for Training of Journalists. Provides training courses across the country which are recognised by newspapers.

NVQs. National Vocational Qualifications. Introduced to give people a chance to gain a universally recognised qualification in their own field of expertise. There are several levels of NVQs with level five being the highest at the time of writing.

Pad out. Writing plenty of background into a story to give it more length.

Page layout. The work carried out by a sub-editor to design a page and add the copy before the paper goes to print.

Paras. Paragraphs.

Press conference. An invitation to the press to attend a gathering where a news item is being announced – like the signing of a new player.

Press pass. A pass needed to get into higher profile sporting events. To gain a press pass you need to apply to the event organisers.

Preview. A piece written before a match looking at what might happen. A preview might include team news, past results and any rivalries.

Processor. The chip in the computer which drives the machine. The more powerful the processor, the faster the machine works.

Remittance slip. A sheet of paper detailing what payments have been made to you – usually by the BACS system.

Reporters. Trained journalists on the staff of a newspaper who cover stories for their publications.

Spike basket. A basket in a computer where all unwanted stories are sent and never seen again.

Sports Council. A body designed to promote sport in the UK by making lottery grants to improve facilities and tempt more people to try out the activity.

Sports editor. The most senior person on a sports desk who makes the ultimate decision on whether they will use your freelance work.

Sub. A shortened term for sub-editor, who is the person who checks through copy and designs page layouts on a daily basis for newspapers.

Sustenance. Food you eat while working away from home on a reporting job. It is claimable against tax.

TEC. Training and Enterprise Council. A group whose aims are to help people train for employment or start their own businesses.

Wapping. The home of the *News of the World* and *The Sun*, the first national papers to leave the renowned birthplace of national newspapers – Fleet Street.

Window. A facility in word processor packages that allows you to have two files open at the same time and flick between the two with a simple mouse command. This is an advantage if you are covering an event for more than one paper and need to write the story in different styles.

Further Reading

BUSINESS MATTERS

Coping with Self Assessment, John Whitely (How To Books, 1999)
Lloyds Bank Tax Guide, Sarah Williams and John Williams (Profile Books, 1998)
Making Money from Writing, Carole Baldock (How To Books, 1998)

IMPROVING YOUR WRITING

Rediscover Grammar, David Crystal (Longman, 1998)
The Kings English, Kingsley Amis (HarperCollins, 1998)
Writing Short Stories and Articles, Adèle Ramet (How To Books, 1998)

EQUIPMENT ADVICE

How To Work from Home, Ian Phillipson (How To Books, second edition 1998)
Living @ Light Speed, Danny Goodman (Arrow, 1995)
Working From Home, S. Gill (HarperCollins, 1996)

HEALTH

Building Self-Esteem, William Stewart (How To Books, 1998)
Managing Your Time, Julie-Ann Amos (How To Books, 1998)
Ten Steps to Energy, Leslie Kenton (Vermilion, 1998)
The Stress Workbook, Joanna Gutmann (Sheldon Press, 1998)
Thriving on Stress, Jan Sutton (How To Books, 1998)

JOURNALISM CONTACTS

The Writer's and Artist's Yearbook, Alex Welsh (A&C Black, 1999)

The Writer's Handbook, Barry Turner (Macmillan, 1999)

SPORTS BOOKS

Footballers Factfile, Barry J. Hugman (Queen Anne Press, 1998)
Playfair Cricket Annual, Bill Frindall (Headline, 1998)
Rothmans Football Yearbook, Glenda Rollin (Headline, 1998)
Rothmans Rugby League Yearbook, Raymond Fletcher, David Howes
  (Headline, 1998)
Rothmans Rugby Union Yearbook, Mick Cleary, John Griffiths
  (Headline, 1998)

LAW

McNae's Essential Law for Journalists, Walter Greenwood and Tom
  Walsh (Butterworth)

Useful Addresses

SPORTS BODIES

The Sports Council, 16 Upper Woburn Place, London WC1H 0QP. Tel: (0171) 273 1500.

The Football Association, 16 Lancaster Gate, London W2 3LW. Tel: (0171) 262 4542.

The Rugby Football Union, Rugby Road, Twickenham, Middlesex TW1 1DZ. Tel: (0181) 892 8161.

The Rugby Football League, Red Hall, Red Hall Lane, Leeds LS17 8NB. Tel: (0113) 232 9111.

RAC Motor Sports Association Ltd, Motor Sports House, Riverside Park, Colnbrook, Slough SL3 0HG. Tel: (01753) 681736.

British Athletic Federation, 225A Bristol Road, Edgbaston, Birmingham B5 7UB. Tel: (0121) 440 5000.

Lawn Tennis Association, The Queens Club, Barons Court, West Kensington, London W14 9EG. Tel: (0171) 381 7000.

English and Wales Cricket Board, Lord's, London NW8 8Q2. Tel: (0171) 432 1200.

JOURNALIST CONTACTS

National Union of Journalists, Acorn House, 314–320 Gray's Inn Road, London WC1X 8DP.

Association of Freelance Journalists, 5 Beacon Flats, Kings Haye Road, Wellington, Telford, Shropshire TF1 1RG.

British Association of Journalists, 88 Fleet Street, London EC4Y 1PJ. Tel: (0171) 353 3003.

National Council for Training of Journalists, Latton Bush Centre, Southern Way, Harlow, Essex CM18 7BL. Tel: (01279) 430009.

The Sports Writers' Association, c/o 16 Upper Woburn Place, London WC1H 0QP.

Index

knowledge, 31, 86

laptops, 26
layout, 86, 87
law, 106–109
Lawton, Matt, 62
libel, 106–108
library, 17, 86

magazines, 19, 35, 48, 101
markets, 35
match programmes, 63
match report, 66
mobile phone, 24
modem, 25, 26, 28
motivation, 121–127
Mullock, Simon, 54
multimedia, 37

NCTJ, 16, 17, 18
Newslink, 28, 74
News of the World, 51, 69
newspapers, 16, 71, 101
Nicoli, Luke, 49
NUJ, 16
NVQ, 17, 18

office, 118, 119
Owen, Michael, 94

payment, 47, 113
PCMICA cards, 30
press association, 35, 65, 73
press box, 63
press conference, 56
press officer, 52, 93
press release, 52, 53
previews, 95
privilege, 60, 107
pyramid, 80

quotes, 71, 83, 109

records, 111
red tops, 20
reference, 31
regional papers, 21, 34, 41
remittance slip, 113
research, 33–39, 61
Reuters, 36
rights, 92
rugby, 93
runner, 66, 67, 73

safety, 118
sales, 103, 104
Self, Jannine, 48
shorthand, 30
spin, 84
Sports Council, 130
sports editor, 34, 41–51
stopwatch, 24
stress, 124
sub-editors, 34, 60
Sun, 20

tabloids, 106, 107
targets, 121
tax, 115
team sheets, 63, 64
TEC, 22
technique, 97
Telegraph, 20
training, 16–22
The Times, 20

websites, 38
weekly papers, 34
workspace, 118
writing groups, 22
writing styles, 21, 82

Zeigler, Martyn, 36